C AMPFIRE STORIES

CHESAPEAKE BAY

T0349260

CAMPFIRE STORIES

CHESAPEAKE BAY

TALES & TRAVEL COMPANION

edited by
ILYSSA KYU & DAVE KYU

MOUNTAINEERS
BOOKS

For our little barnacle and seal, Lula and Isla.
We'll always be your rock.

MOUNTAINEERS BOOKS is dedicated
to the exploration, preservation, and enjoyment of
outdoor and wilderness areas.

1001 SW Klickitat Way, Suite 201, Seattle, WA 98134
800-553-4453, www.mountaineersbooks.org

Copyright © 2025 by Ilyana Kim and Dave Kyu

Printed in China

28 27 26 25   1 2 3 4 5

Design and layout: Melissa McFeeters

Library of Congress Cataloging-in-Publication data is on file for this title at
https://lccn.loc.gov/2024947842

Mountaineers Books titles may be purchased for corporate, educational, or other
promotional sales, and our authors are available for a wide range of events. For
information on special discounts or booking an author, contact our customer
service at 800-553-4453 or mbooks@mountaineersbooks.org.

Printed on FSC®-certified materials

ISBN (paperback): 978-1-68051-752-1
ISBN (ebook): 978-1-68051-753-8

An independent nonprofit publisher since 1960

Contents

EXPLORE THE CHESAPEAKE BAY

A Bay Bound by Collective Action

THE CHESAPEAKE BAY is the largest estuary in the United States, comprising of wetlands, marshes, tributaries, and bay waters that are home and hunting grounds for blue crab, oysters, and striped bass (called rockfish here)—along with ospreys, eagles, waterfowl, and other migratory birds. With more than 150 freshwater rivers and streams entering from six states—Delaware, Maryland, New York, Pennsylvania, Virginia, and West Virginia—and the District of Columbia, here is a place where fresh and salt water mix into a brackish bay offering just the right salinity, temperature, depth, and flow to form one of the most productive and biodiverse ecosystems on this planet. It's a place where fresh- and saltwater creatures coexist, serving as a nursery and migratory stopover for all kinds of marine life and waterfowl.

In fact, it has done so for millennia—the Chesapeake was part of a warm and shallow sea ten to twenty million years ago. Today you can visit massive Calvert Cliffs, once the shoreline of this ancient sea, where erosion reveals its rich biodiversity in the form of shark teeth, shells, and fossils of ancient whales, rays, birds, and crocodiles.

The Chesapeake Bay watershed has the largest land-to-water ratio of any coastal water body in the world, 14:1. Beyond the bay itself, more than a hundred thousand streams, creeks, and rivers—the largest being the James, Potomac, Rappahannock, Susquehanna, and York Rivers—weave through 64,000 square miles of watershed. This watershed is a lot of things to a lot of people who live in it—a beautiful landscape to admire; a shoreline to explore while walking or biking; a refreshing body of water for swimming, fishing, or paddling; a source of drinking water; and perhaps most notably, a hugely important part of the local economy. A huge population of people living around the Chesapeake Bay make their living from the 348 species of finfish and 173 of shellfish that inhabit it. Five hundred million pounds of seafood, totaling $2.8 billion in sales, are harvested each year by an industry that provides twenty thousand jobs.

Ask any local what defines the Chesapeake, and it generally revolves around the seafood industry, which in so many ways has shaped the culture, the community, and people's connection to this place. Plenty of locals we met still remember when oysters and crabs were so plentiful they could walk down to the docks and harvest them for dinner with minimal effort. But the health of the Bay and its bounty have declined drastically due to commercial overfishing, disease, pollution, and climate change, leading to a palpable sense of anxiety and loss in the region.

More than eighteen million people call the Chesapeake Bay watershed home, and several major cities, including Washington DC and Baltimore, have an impact on the Bay's water quality, wildlife, and habitats. When we spoke with the team at the Alliance for the Chesapeake Bay, we quickly learned that you can't talk about the Bay without talking about what's happening upstream. Some of the biggest threats to the health of the Chesapeake include runoff from agricultural, urban, and suburban areas; runoff from hazardous waste sites and treatment plants; and pollutants deposited by rain, snow, and fog. Contaminants include nitrogen, phosphorus, and toxic chemicals that are washed into local streams and rivers, and from there into the Bay. These cloud and pollute the water, trigger algae blooms, alter the oxygen balance, and leave waterways without the ability to support the biodiverse aquatic life of the Bay and its tributaries.

Two hundred years ago, the Bay's massive oyster reefs supported millions of "filter feeders" like oysters, which cleaned the water, allowing early explorers to see 3 fathoms, or 18 feet, down into healthy water. That's not the case today, but there's hope for recovery. The alliance aims to prevent pollution by networking and collaborating with organizations, communities, and agencies throughout the region, and by educating farmers, land owners, residents, and business owners about how the chemicals they use on their farms, gardens, driveways, and landscapes impact the Chesapeake Bay, hundreds of miles downstream. "There are 18.5 million people who wake up one to two hours away from the Bay itself," a member of the team told us, "and they're the ones who need to make changes." Some may also need a new perspective. One local resident explained to us that at one time many homes along the Bay's shoreline had few or no windows on the water side, because residents wanted to avoid looking at the "factory" in their backyard. Many still remember the Bay's dead zones—the floating dead fish, the dead birds washed ashore, and the green and brown algae blooms that advertised how sick this body of water was.

To connect to the water beyond taste buds and paychecks, people need *access* to it, and that can be challenging around the Chesapeake. When we visit a place for research, the first thing we do is immerse ourselves in the natural environment, but here we were surprised to find ourselves having a hard time finding places to access the shoreline. When we wondered out loud if we had missed something in our planning, Jody Couser, who works with the Chesapeake Conservancy, nodded and validated that recreating on the water here is not easy. The 11,684-mile-long bay shoreline is desirable real estate parceled out into private and commercial land with just a handful of parks reserved for the public to paddle, swim, relax, or stroll.

Most people experience the Chesapeake by way of the highways and roads to and around it, but Jody notes that your perspective changes when you experience it by boat. For a large part of the human history of the Chesapeake Bay, that was the primary way of exploring its many rivers, streams, and creeks. Today, however, accessing the water has become a privilege for those wealthy enough to own watercraft or charter a boat, and then find one of the few locations where they can launch it. Jody told us about meeting a videographer for National Geographic who lives in Washington, DC and has traveled all over the world, yet found himself setting his feet in the Chesapeake Bay—his home turf—for the very first time while filming ospreys at Sandy Point.

This disconnect between ordinary people and the shoreline of the Chesapeake is what inspired Jody to document her visits to 123 beaches on her blog *Chesapeake Beaches*. It's also part of what motivates the campaign for a Chesapeake National Recreation Area (CNRA), which would allow the region to leverage the resources of the National Park Service to improve public access to the Bay, enhance the visitor experience, offer interpretive and educational materials and programs highlighting the Bay's rich history, and protect the natural environment. According to the people we met, a CNRA would make it easier for the public to get out on the water, an important step toward helping people form a connection to the Chesapeake and getting them to take action at home or in their communities.

Beyond the economic and recreational allures of Chesapeake Bay, the region holds interest due to the depth of human history here. Jody told us, "Traveling the Chesapeake Bay takes you through every layer of American history—here, you're traveling the history of the nation and in ways, the birthplace of American identity, so it's a unique opportunity to relate to history in the present day." But as author and geologist Lauret Savoy has pointed out in her article "Ancestral Structures on the Trailing Edge," the Chesapeake's history is not without its dark shadows: "Vestiges of repeated geologic collision, rupture, and erosion fill this broad Chesapeake-Appalachian terrain. Human forms of collision, rupture, and erosion occurred here as well. Looming as heavy shadows are traces of a history foundational to the United States and to what the nation would become. Traces that still mark each of us in this country today. The region witnessed perhaps the oldest lengthy convergence of peoples from Indigenous North America, Africa, and Europe in what would come to be called the thirteen British colonies."

With its vast network of waterways and its location on the border of the slave-holding southern colonies, the Chesapeake region has a key place in Black American history. The first enslaved Africans arrived in Jamestown, Virginia, 60 miles up the James River from the Chesapeake Bay, in 1619. By 1780, one-third of the Chesapeake population were indentured servants. But as a border state, Virginia was also home to free Black citizens and many sympathetic white citizens. Harriet Tubman used the

Underground Railroad's robust "Chesapeake Station," a network of safe houses accessed through the waterways in this region, to lead enslaved Black people to freedom. Frederick Douglass, also born into slavery, watched sailing ships from the eastern banks of the Chesapeake and dreamed of freedom; eventually he became a powerful advocate against slavery. After the Civil War settling into a free society, Black laborers worked as watermen: building boats, catching oysters, and processing each day's catch.

In the era of Jim Crow laws, Black travelers in areas like New Jersey's Ocean City or Atlantic City risked being denied hotel rooms, auto repair, or access to leisure activities like walking on a public beach. Chesapeake's history, in contrast, created a safe space for them. Black Americans flocked to Carr's, Sparrow's, and Elktonia Beaches on the Chesapeake, where they were welcome. Music venues sprang up and hosted renowned Black musicians like Billie Holiday, Ray Charles, and Little Richard as part of the "Chitlin Circuit."

A Chesapeake National Recreation Area, Jody shared with us, could connect people to these rich and forgotten histories. She helped us imagine a future where electric ferries take visitors to sites that share the area's diverse history, while a new interpretive center focuses on highlighting stories that often go untold in the Chesapeake region, including those of free and enslaved Blacks, the Indigenous tribes of this region, and the waterwomen who were an essential part of the region's successful seafood industry and contributed to the thriving economy and the health of the Bay. Another effort to lift up forgotten history has been led by Vincent O. Leggett, who founded the Blacks of the Chesapeake (BOC) project in 1984 to preserve the history of the unique role of Black ship captains, sail makers, watermen, and seafood processing plant employees in shaping the Chesapeake.

Long before Europeans arrived, the Chesapeake Bay region was—and still remains—the homeland to many tribes, all of whom were represented by three chiefdoms: the Powhatan (including the Powhatan, Pamunkey, and other tribes), the Piscataway (including the Patapsco, Patuxent, and other tribes), and the Nanticoke (including the Choptank, Doeg, and other tribes). The region between the Chesapeake Bay and the Potomac River was home to the Piscataway peoples, among the largest and most powerful tribes in the region. In the Algonquin language, the word Piscataway translates to "where the waters blend," which according to Dr. Gabrielle Tayac, historian and enrolled member of the Piscataway Indian Nation, refers to the location of their capital village of Moyaone at the confluence of the Potomac River and Piscataway Creek in present-day Maryland.

Dr. Tayac refers to the Potomac as "a vein of Mother Earth's lifeblood." The river nurtured the Indigenous populations that for thousands of years would move through the Chesapeake Bay region to hunt and fish in balance with the abundant gifts of the environment. When English colonists settled in Jamestown, Virginia, in 1607, tribal leaders saw a trade opportunity and taught the colonizers how to farm, even offering permission to live on their territorial lands. But conflicts and new diseases like smallpox, cholera, and measles devastated the Indigenous populations. The Piscataway saw their estimated eighty-five hundred members in 1600 reduced to three hundred in just a century. Greatly weakened, the tribes signed treaties to move onto smaller reservation lands in exchange for peace and the right to hunt, only to see these treaties ignored after their resettlement.

In order to survive, many tribal members assimilated into European culture during a period that Chief Anne Richardson of the Rappahannock tribe describes as the silent years, when tribespeople "went underground because of English encroachment and racial oppression, [and] hid out in various places." As a result of more recent activism, tribes today have been able to reclaim some of their ancestral lands. In 2012, after decades of lobbying, the Piscataway Conoy Tribe and the Piscataway Indian Nation were recognized by the State of Maryland. Contemporary tribes have started projects to reintroduce their language, their traditions, and their heritage to a new generation in hopes of restoring the special balance their people once had with the land here.

The restoration of tribal knowledge and culture isn't the only encouraging thing we discovered around the Chesapeake Bay—but it took us some time. Truth be told, the Chesapeake's difficult history, its loss of culture and heritage, its declining species, and its disappearing islands left us feeling like sad trombones during our visit. As we drove around, we saw abundant evidence that climate change is not just coming; it's already here. Streets that end at or run parallel to the water are flooded indefinitely. Swampy front yards and driveways seem to have become part of the Bay, which creeps toward waterlogged houses, sagging and windswept. Ghost forests hug shorelines where rising sea levels overwhelm tree roots with salt water, killing stands of oak and loblolly pine, pushing forests back fifteen feet a year and accelerating. We wondered if we even *could* create a collection we were excited by, one that would help people connect with this hard-to-access landscape.

Despite all of this, in our conversations with people around the Bay, we found abundant hope and beauty. We heard *lots* of stories of collective action motivated by a love for the landscape and its complex history—and saw evidence that it's working. Oyster reefs and native plants, which provide safe harbor for many of the Bay's iconic species like blue crab, are rebounding. The coalitions that work to educate and engage people around the Bay are empowering residents to become volunteers, activists, and citizen scientists. This work is bolstered by businesses, corporations, and state agencies in an all-hands-in effort that sets an example to the world for how to clean up a watershed.

People are even beginning to swim in the waterways again, an activity once deemed a health hazard. The Anacostia River, once so polluted it would catch fire, is now so dramatically improved that in 2023, swimming was permitted for the first time in fifty years for the inaugural Anacostia Riverkeeper *Splash!* event. And in Baltimore, a decades-long effort to make the once-neglected Inner Harbor swimmable again paid off in 2024, when the Waterfront Partnership of Baltimore hosted the Harbor Splash event in which 150 people jumped into the harbor for a swim—a hopeful first step toward more water-focused activities like open water swimming, paddleboarding, and beach recreation. These are hopeful messages not to give up, but also reminders that such opportunities don't make themselves—it really does come down to a community-wide effort of pitching in, advocating, and working together to seed lasting change for current and future generations. As one person put it, "The Chesapeake Bay is on the rebound. It's slow and incremental, but it's a story of optimism—a place where partners from every angle of society have come together to do work and restore the Bay."

The short stories, personal essays, and poems in this collection are intended to capture the spirit and rich history of the Chesapeake Bay. They're meant to be read around a "fire"—whether quietly to yourself from the comfort of your couch or aloud to the people sharing the ember glow of a campfire with you. These are not stories for those seeking just to be entertained with classic spooky stories, but were collected instead for those who are curious about how this special region came to be and why it continues to mean so much to us—because the stories we tell shape our values and our future.

Our *Campfire Stories* collections typically feature naturecentered stories, but in the case of the Chesapeake Bay, nature and industry are inextricably linked. The Chesapeake is defined not just by its landscape but also by its history—what we can learn from it and what we can accomplish when we join together with a shared purpose. *This is the spirit of the Chesapeake. The stories in this book will teach you about species of marine life caught here and consumed across the country, as well as the people who harvest them. You will learn about the rituals, traditions, and heritage of watermen and waterwomen; the watercraft and tools, like dredge boats, skipjacks, and tongers, designed for fishing; the history of those enslaved here and their deep knowledge of the land, which helped lead them to freedom; and the complex mixing of water, wildlife, and plant life that makes this region so bountiful and unique.

To identify themes and stories for this collection, we interviewed individuals who live and work here. We spent many days inside libraries and bookstores along the Bay, and visited the region's shores, tributaries, pine forests, marshes, and crab houses, its rich natural and cultural landmarks. We sought recommendations and insights from locals and combined them with our own experiences to create a guide to visiting this special place— practical tips on where to go, what to do, and where to camp, as well as ideas on how to visit in ways that respect and support the resident communities, human and wild.

We walk away from our time in the Chesapeake and our reading of these stories with a feeling of resilience and hope—inspired by those who so boldly have demonstrated the power of collective action. It's our wish that this collection describing the wonders of the Bay will deepen your connection to the region, whether you live here, have visited a hundred times, or only know the Bay through the pages of this book, and inspire us all to make changes for the good of the whole. So suit up and jump into the Chesapeake waters with us!

Storytelling Tips

Storytelling has always been a fundamental part of being human. Beyond entertainment, stories have allowed us to share knowledge, traditions, and ideas, and to feel a sense of connection with people and places beyond our own experiences for thousands of years.

Through all its forms, we have witnessed how stories can create deeper emotional connections between people and the natural world. This is especially true across generations and communities who have been disconnected from the outdoors, yet who are, increasingly, responsible for protecting it.

We believe that stories are best when they're shared with others, so we encourage you to share any stories or sections you love with friends or family, continuing in the tradition of oral storytelling, by sharing them aloud.

Should you find yourself gathered with others around a campfire, here are some tips for sharing a story:

Be prepared. A campfire can provide a warm, flickering light that sets the perfect mood but may not be adequate for reading a book, so bring a lantern, flashlight, headlamp, or book light. A glass of water can rescue you from a fit of coughing or a dry mouth, so keep it handy. In a camp setting with crickets and a crackling fire, you may be competing to be heard—sit or stand up straight, breathe from your diaphragm, and project your voice.

Choose the right story. Select a story that matches your audience's interests, age, attention span, and the moment. Pay attention to length; if it's too long, consider summarizing and read aloud only a particularly interesting or engaging poem or passage.

Introduce the story. Explain why you want to read this story, what it's about, and who wrote it—keeping it short and sweet. (Feel free to use our insider knowledge from the "About This Story" sections to get your audience excited.) End with a thought about what you took away from it and a question to engage your listeners.

Bring the story alive. Every story, especially poetry, has its own rhythm. When you read aloud, read it slightly faster than you would naturally speak but without rushing. Keep your listeners' attention by breaking up the rhythm with a long pause or a different cadence. (But don't overuse this trick or overperform!) Be authentic, enunciate clearly, and let your natural reactions enhance the story without disrupting the flow.

Most of all, have fun! Whether reading this book around a campfire, in your living room, at a park, or tucked cozily in bed, we hope you will find something that makes the natural world come alive.

She's the Mother of the waters and the people of this land;
forty river children reach to take her by the hand,
and flow through Maryland and Virginia to the sea.
She's Atlantic born, Atlantic bound and free.

✦

—TOM WISNER,
CHESAPEAKE BORN

CHESAPEAKE BAY

STORIES

The Bay

WILLIAM W. WARNER

Excerpt from *Beautiful Swimmers*

t is so known through the length and breadth of its watershed. The Bay. There is no possible confusion with any other body of water, no need for more precise description. It is, after all, the continent's largest estuary. Its waters are rich, the main supply of oysters, crabs, clams and other seafoods for much of the Atlantic seaboard. Its shorelines cradled our first settlements. It is the Chesapeake.

North to south, from the choppy wavelets of the Susquehanna Flats to the rolling surges of the Virginia capes, the Bay measures almost exactly two hundred miles. Alone among its vital statistics, its breadth is not impressive. The extremes are four miles near Annapolis and about thirty miles near the mouth of the Potomac River. In all else the Bay is champion. Its shoreline is prodigious. Put together the great rivers on its western shore: the York, the James, the Susquehanna and the Potomac. Add the labyrinthine marshlands of the Eastern Shore, always capitalized, since it is a land unto itself. The combined shorelines string out to about 4,000 miles, or more than enough to cross the country at its widest. Some say the figure doubles if all tributaries are followed beyond the reach of the tide. The Bay's entire watershed extends north through Pennsylvania to the Finger Lakes and Mohawk Valley country of New York, by virtue of the Susquehanna, the mother river that created the Bay in Pleistocene time. To the west it traces far back into the furrowed heartland of Appalachia, but one mountain ridge short of the Ohio-Mississippi drainage, by agency of the Potomac. To the east the flatland rivers of the Eastern Shore rise from gum and oak thickets almost within hearing distance of the pounding surf of the Atlantic barrier islands. To the south, Bay waters seep through wooded swamps to the North Carolina sounds, where palmettos, alligators and great stands of bald cypress first appear.

To qualify as an estuary, a body of water must be well enclosed, provide easy entry and exit for open sea water and enjoy a vigorous infusion of fresh water from one or more rivers. These are minimum requirements. The fjords of Norway are estuaries, but they are uniformly rocky, deep and thus biologically impoverished, which is why Norwegian fishermen spend most of their time on offshore banks. A good estuary with high biological productivity requires other things. Shallow water, for one, which the sun can penetrate to nourish both plankton and rooted aquatic plants. Extensive marshland is another. An estuary without it lacks the lacework of tidal creeks and shallow coves which traps nutrients and protects and feeds the larvae and juveniles of a host of fish and invertebrates.

Also, to be summa cum laude in estuarine productivity, there must be circulation. A good mix, one is tempted to say, is almost everything. Not just in one direction. There should be two-layered or horizontal circulation in which heavier salt water from the ocean slides under the lighter and fresher surface water from rivers. Inexorably, that is, with a net flow upstream on the bottom and downstream on the top which surmounts the temporary effects of wind and tide. Ideally, there should also be some vertical mixing, which is not found in every estuary, since it requires significant contrasts in depths and water temperatures.

By all tests the Chesapeake does well. Its very configuration, its long north-south axis, encourages and concentrates horizontal or two-layered circulation. The result is a splendid salinity gradation or, to be more exact, twenty-five parts salt per thousand of water down near the Virginia capes, which is almost ocean, to zero or fresh water at the northern or upper end of the Bay. Fresh water infusion is constant and indeed vigorous. Often, in fact, it is too much of a good thing, as when the rivers of the western shore rise in spring foods. Mightiest of these is the Susquehanna, the longest river of the eastern seaboard. Next in order along the Bay's western shore come the Potomac, James, Rappahannock, York and Patuxent....

Vertical mixture takes place thanks mainly to a deep channel running almost the total length of the Bay. Geomorphologically speaking, it is the fossilized bed of the ancient Susquehanna. It lies at the bottom of the Bay at depths of eighty to one hundred and twenty feet, still well defined after 15,000 years of silting and sedimentation. In its first life it was the course of an upstart river searching and scouring its way to the sea, nourished by Pleistocene glaciers not far to the north. As glaciers melted in the post-Pleistocene, rising ocean waters drowned the river valley to create the Bay much as we know it now. Today ship captains running to Baltimore know the old river well; it is the route of seagoing commerce. Trouble is in store for those who don't or who ignore the pilot's warnings. Its shoulders are sharp, and sure stranding attends any deviation from course.

To the Bay's host of marine organisms the fossil river is equally important. In late summer and early fall fresh seawater—fresh in the sense of oxygen content—creeps in along its bottom and branches up the tributaries with unusual strength, since rivers are low and their obstructing flow weak. Above it lies tired or biologically exhausted water. All summer long the surface waters have supported immense communities of plankton, not to mention sometimes harmful algae, greedily consuming oxygen. Now these waters are oxygen-starved. But it is autumn and they are cooling more rapidly than the deep water below. Being heavier, they sink. Conversely, the intruding seawater below carrying fresh oxygen slowly begins to rise. The mix is thus two-way. In the process the microscopic plant and animal plankton, heavily concentrated near the surface in summer, are swirled up and down and thus distributed more uniformly. Some of the Bay's most prominent year-round residents—the blue crab, the striped bass, the white perch—take their cue and make rapidly for the deeps. There they can feed amid the deeper groves of plankton and enjoy warmer water as autumn slowly turns to winter. (Theoretically, oysters and clams would do well to follow suit, but locomotion, alas, is not within their powers.) Crabs especially appreciate the deep water in autumn, since it prolongs the time left to them before cold water will force virtual hibernation in the post-Pleistocene ooze. The great channel is therefore a winter haven, a place for rest and limited feeding free of the temperature extremes of surface waters.

In spring vertical mixing again takes place through reversal of the autumn factors. Reoxygenation starts at the surface. In response the fish ascend and the crabs start a slow and measured crawl up out of the channel. The crabs' eventual goal is the shoal areas where eelgrass abounds and where the new spring water courses over the shallows with every tide. They go there to hide and to feed and to feel the rays of the warming sun. And think about other things associated with spring.

"Feller hasn't run ashore, he don't much know this Bay," a waterman once said to me after he pulled my ketch off a tenacious sandbar. It was the nicest thing anyone could possibly say under such embarrassing circumstances and it made me feel much better. What he meant, of course, is that the Chesapeake does not lack for the shallow water that is another prime estuarine requirement. The average depth of the Chesapeake, mother river and tributary channels included, is twenty-one feet. For most of the Bay, fifteen feet or less would be a better figure.

Shallower still are vast areas along the Eastern Shore, the waters surrounding the great marsh islands of Tangier Sound, for example, which Captain John Smith called the Isles of Limbo, where vigorous sounding will fail to uncover anything deeper than five feet. Captain Smith was glad when he left, and today's less venturesome sailors shun the marshy islands like the plague. Yet these very shoal waters have their place, if not for yachtsmen. They provide an optimum habitat for such rooted aquatic plants as wild celery and widgeongrass, the choice of waterfowl, or eelgrass and sea lettuce, which although acceptable to ducks and geese, are only preferred by small fish, crabs and young seed oysters. Almost invariably the shoals supporting these water plants are bordered by marsh. The marshlands in turn support a much greater growth of plants, plants which want to have their roots covered by water some of the time, but cannot tolerate it all of the time. Dominating these, heavily outweighing all other species in sheer tonnage and outdistancing them in distribution, are the spiky *Spartinas* or cord-grasses. *Spartina patens*, that is, which ripples in windrows or lies in natural cowlicks on the firmer ground, and *Spartina alterniflora*, taller and denser, which grows on the quaking mudbanks and along creek borders first invaded by tidewater. . . .

Down every tidal gut and through every big "thorofare" and little "swash" or "drain," as the breaks in the marsh islands are called, there comes an enormous and nourishing flow of silage made from this decomposing *Spartina* crop. Waiting to receive the flow, well protected by wavy forests of eelgrass, are many forms of life. First recipients are plankton and the larvae and young of larger forms, who need it most. In the latter category are enormous infant populations of fish, clams, oysters, jellyfish and worms. Predominant among adult forms are the blue crabs, who have a fine time of it preying on the small fry, including, sometimes, some of their own. . . .

Most of the Chesapeake's *Spartina* marsh is concentrated on the lower Eastern Shore in a broad belt extending south from Maryland's Little Choptank River. "South of the Little Choptank," the watermen tell you, "the fast land disappears." It is their way of saying that only isolated islands or small clumps of firm ground dot the vast marsh landscape of these parts. The larger islands are called hammocks; often they support whole fishing villages or a considerable growth of pine and hardwoods. The smaller ones, with barely enough soil to nourish a single bush or tree, are dismissed as "tumps." Seen from the air, the region appears very much like an Everglades of the north. It is the largest undisturbed marshland in the mid-Atlantic states, undisturbed because it is far from ocean beaches and thus largely overlooked by developers. May it remain so.

Such are the Bay's estuarine assets. Each makes its contribution and together they combine to produce marketable marine resources of incredible volume. The Maryland portion of the Bay alone produces more oysters than any other state in the union, with an annual harvest of approximately three million bushels. (Jurisdiction of the Chesapeake is divided; Virginia controls 985 square miles of Bay waters and Maryland 703.) Together the two Bay states supply one-quarter of the United States' oyster catch, worth about $22,000,000 dockside. Since its inception in the 1950s, the Bay's soft or "steamer" clam industry has provided over half the national catch of this species, moving all of New England to second rank.

But it is in the stocks of the familiar Atlantic blue crab that the Bay's bounty stretches belief. No body of water in the world has been more intensively fished for crabs than the Chesapeake, nor for a longer period, with such successful result. Since its beginning in the mid-nineteenth century, the Bay's blue crab fishery has made the United States the leading crab-consuming nation of the world, followed closely by Japan only in recent years. . . .

Blue crabs are now fished commercially from Delaware Bay down the Atlantic seaboard to Florida and around into the Gulf Coast as far as Louisiana and Texas. The biggest catch by far comes from the Chesapeake Bay. The Bay annually offers up anywhere from fifty to eighty million pounds in poor years and good years respectively, or approximately half the total catch of the species. This means that anywhere from 150 to 240 million individual blue crabs are removed from the Bay waters each year, since the average market specimen weighs one-third of a pound. Not only that, our dependence on the Chesapeake for the succulent soft crab is almost total or ninety-five percent of the national catch in this form. This is not a matter of biology or habitat, but human industry. Skill, hard work and infinite patience are required to hold crabs in "Aloats" or pens until they moult and successfully bring them live to market. People in other places don't want to do it. Only the Core Sound area of North Carolina, where early season softs are a short-term specialty prior to the opening of the shrimp season, and certain localities in Florida and the Gulf states, where there is a local restaurant trade, are exceptions. Practically speaking, therefore, but for the strong work ethic of Chesapeake watermen this most delectable form of crab would never come to market.

As might be expected, the Chesapeake's grand mixtures of fresh and salt water are also ideal for anadromous fishes, or those that spend part of their life in the sea and part far up estuaries for spawning and early growth. Most prized by both sport and commercial fishermen is the striped bass, always called rockfish in the Bay country. Here again honors go to Maryland. Its fresher half of the Bay regularly leads all other states with an annual catch of four to five million pounds. . . .

The Bay has other treasures, not all at the head of lists. Enormous herring runs, sufficient to support a sizable canning industry and provide the herring roe Virginians like to eat for breakfast with scrambled eggs. Mink, muskrat, nutria and otter, sad to include, trapped in the lovely marshes of Maryland's Dorchester County, in numbers second only to Louisiana. Sky-darkening flocks of migrating and wintering waterfowl, in the thickest concentrations of the Atlantic flyway.

Enough superlatives. They mislead. The Chesapeake does not impress those who know it best as the grandest or most of anything. For all its size and gross statistics, it is an intimate place where land and water intertwine in infinite varieties of mood and pattern. None has captured the essential Bay better than its principal discoverer, Captain John Smith. After rounding the sand dunes of Capes Charles and Henry, he wrote:

> *a faire Bay compassed but for the mouth with fruitful
> and delightsome land. Within is a country that may have
> the prerogative over the most pleasant places of Europe,
> Asia, Africa or America, for large and pleasant navigable
> rivers. Heaven and earth never agreed better to frame a
> place for man's habitation.*

Although more than one historian has called the doughty explorer America's first press agent, none has seriously suggested that he was far off the mark in his description of the Chesapeake. It is true, of course, that ice occasionally grips the Bay, and winter storms are not unknown. The summer thunder squalls (and sometimes waterspouts) are notorious. A prominent yachtsman who has sailed the world oceans once told me he had never been so taken by surprise, dragged anchor farther, or felt more helpless than when hit by a fast-moving thunderstorm off Oxford, Maryland, in the month of July. But for most of the time the mood of the Bay is gentle and charitable. There are no rocks to claw or rend ship bottoms. Tidal range is slight and currents, when found, are more a refreshing diversion than an obstacle. Fog is rare. Caught in an autumn gale, the prudent skipper knows that he need only run a short distance before the storm to find a wide choice of snug, completely enclosed anchorages, where gallery forests of pine and oak come down to the water's edge and where geese and wild swan still fly over at masthead height with every dawn.

Delightsome, fruitful, pleasant. So it is, most would say, to this day.

About This Story

Before we came to the Chesapeake, we conflated the idea of an estuary with *sanctuary*, which is not entirely wrong. But as we learned more, we became fascinated by how unique the layers, mixing, and composition of these waters are. Estuaries are enclosed bodies of water where freshwater rivers meet the sea—transition zones between land and sea that play a critical role as feeding, nursing, and resting grounds for all kinds of life. In fact, they serve as nurseries for more than 75 percent of the fish we catch. Not only do they filter the water and reduce pollution, but they also protect our shorelines and communities from flooding.

While the bulk of William Warner's Pulitzer Prize–winning book *Beautiful Swimmers: Watermen, Crabs and the Chesapeake Bay* focuses on the region's mascot—*Callinectes sapidus*, the blue crab—and the watermen who seek it, this passage helps us understand the minutia and complexity of this vast body of water where the blue crab thrives. Just in terms of scale, the Chesapeake Bay is the largest estuary in the United States, touching and receiving freshwater from six states—Delaware, Maryland, New York, Pennsylvania, Virginia, West Virginia—and the District of Columbia. We love how this passage highlights all that makes this place so biologically special, focusing on the details that are easy to overlook in the industrialization of these waters.

Estuary, the Chesapeake Bay

LARA PAYNE

Bounded. Boundaried.
There are other ways of knowing your place
but this is my way:

slow quiet waves a steady monotony
almost hush. Never silent.
At night I wonder, is it my ears or the ocean?

Though not an ocean, here,
nor sea but an estuary, salt water
and brackish. How many fresh

waters rush to make this great
cradle? Blue crabs, oysters, eel grass
rockfish and shad. Things that crawl

and filter. Oysters take cloudy water
turn it clear. He taught me early
how to take the shell

and tear it away to reach the gleaming
 meat. "This is the Capitol Building
so it is female, this is the Washington

Monument so it is male." The shape
of their sex is the space I will place
the tips of my thumbs to open

with a crack the body of the blue now red crab.
Later a similar man though not family
showed me how to take a blunt knife to open

the oyster. "Gently, almost quietly"
he warned, "and then quick, But hold
your palm flat to catch all

of the oyster's brine." If my eyes
leak the same water as this,
will sand collect in your palm

About This Story

Marshy Point Nature Center sits on the edge of a large concentration
of productive wetlands just outside of Baltimore. Open from sunrise
to sunset every day, it is accessible to a dense urban population by
train and bus. For many people, this is their first introduction to a
wetland or estuary, and it's one of the only places in this region where
you can stand out on the pier and, aside from a modest boathouse,
see only nature, despite being flanked entirely by suburbs, towns,
and cities. Not many residents share the intimate connection to and
knowledge of the Bay demonstrated in this poem by Lara Payne, who

has lived near the Chesapeake's tributaries for nearly her whole life. Places like Marshy Point play an important role in helping people form meaningful connections with the land through interactive exhibits, programs, trails, and various outdoor experiences.

Beyond being just a delicious delicacy, oysters are essentially miniature water treatment plants filtering sediment, algae, nitrogen, and phosphorus from the water. One oyster can filter fifty gallons of water per day. Early explorers found clean, clear bay waters thanks to a diverse and abundant system of oyster reefs, but disease, human impact, and climate change have since decimated the once-healthy oyster population. At Marshy Point, we stumbled upon reef balls, concrete domes with holes emulating an oyster reef structure, designed to provide a hard surface for oysters to settle and grow on, and serve as a habitat for fish, crabs, and other marine organisms. The hope is that these artificial reefs placed in the Bay can help repopulate the reef and restore the ecosystem to what it was in the 1600s, when Captain John Smith observed that oyster beds "lay as thick as stones."

We first came across Payne's poem in the exhibition *The Changing Chesapeake* at the Chesapeake Bay Maritime Museum in St. Michaels, Maryland. Local artists were prompted to reflect on these topics: how climate change and the impact of humans on the environment shape their community, how the way they identify with and are inspired by the Chesapeake has evolved, what they would want someone a hundred years from now to know about life and community traditions, and their vision for the future of life in the region. Payne's hope for a hundred years from now? That "we will continue to treasure and protect the Chesapeake."

These Chesapeake Men

GILBERT BYRON

From Chesapeake men I come,
These men a sun-tanned, quiet breed,
With eyes of English blue and faces
Lined with many a watch of sunlit waters;
These men with cautious mouths and lazy stride,
Grizzled-chinned, hip-booted, oil skinned men;
These men, they fear the Chesapeake,
And yet they would not leave her.

Down to the bay they go,
Top-sailed schooner, one-masted skipjack,
Canoe-sterned bugeye, sails full;
Rowing a garvey, sculling a skiff,
Poling a scow, and, if they must—
Pounding along in a bateau powered
With a one cylinder engine.

They seek the imperial shad and the lowly crab,
The oyster, the weakfish, the turtle, the rockfish,
The muskrat, the eel, the terrapin, diamondbacked,
The clam, the blue fish, the wild duck—
And food for their souls
Which they sometimes find.

In the calling of the wild duck,
In the mating of the kingfisher,
In the sloughing of the soft crab,
In the softness of the water's touch
In the flight of great blue heron,
In the sculling of the oar,
In the passing schools of fish,
In the belly of the sail,
In the hauling of the seine,
In the taste of oysters raw,
In the soaring fish-hawk's wings,
In the touch of southwest wind,
In the little waves that break,
In the surge against the prow,
In the cliffs of yellow clay
In the setting of the sun,
In the quest of quiet harbor—
In the Chesapeake.

The Fullest Moon

GILBERT BYRON

There she lies,
An old white schooner
Rotting in the sun.
Her course is run,
The last harbor reached,
Beached on a yellow sand-bar.
Her captain, the stern-eyed fish-hawk,
A wily shitepoke mate,
And crew of swaggering, fiddler crabs.
So quiet now,
She only moves
When the full moon
And the flood tide
Cause her to stir
And rise with memories
Of windy days.
Perhaps someday her master
When the fullest moon shall rise,
Will muster his scuttling knaves
And sail her down the bay,

To find a grave
In deeper waves.

Long ago fall storms
Washed most of her planks away;
The tides stole the oakum and pitch
Which filled her seams;
Last year's hurricane
Brought the foremast down
To rest across
Her clipper bow;
Her rigging etched upon
An evening sky
Brings a sigh

To all whose loving hands
Have ever snugged
A mainsail down.
A lone deadeye,
A shackle there,
An iron cleat,
A wooden block,
Tell little of
The sail she carried
Or the tale
Her wake could tell.

She was born on the Eastern Shore,
White oak for her straight keel,
Locust knees and curved stem,

Heart of white oak,
Sheathed her frame,
Seasoned seven years.
The birds gave up their trees,
The tallest yellow pines,
For her tallowed, white- tipped masts.
Sawdust and oak chips,
Adze strokes and iron spikes,
Caulking mallet pounding oakum,
Hot pitch to pay the seams,
These were her flesh.
Then great bolts of snowy canvas,
Sail twine, the wedge-shaped needle,
Tarred rope with marlin served,
Sewed grommets and the cringle,
Brass sheaves within the blocks,
Hemp rope belaying pins,
Deadeyes laced with plow-wire tense,
Brought the spirit.

Lazy-jacks and topping lifts,
Bower anchors and iron chain
Wound around the windlass drum,
Curved davits and the yawl boat,
Foot-ropes and halyards rove,
Painted guibre under bowsprit,
She waits a breeze.

How white and fresh she is
Sliding down the ways.

Down she goes,
Down the Chester, the Choptank,
    the Sassafras,
Down the Wicomico, the Elk, the Potomac,
Down the Tred Avon,
Down the Bohemia,
Down the Chesapeake.
Carrying wheat, whole wheat,
In a clean, sweet hold,
Not in bags,
But yellow kernels
Rolling down
A smooth board.
Her decks lined
With baskets of red tomatoes;
Her broad decks sheathed
With rough boards,
Piled with oysters,
Piled with crabs,
So soon to find
A new shell,
A machine-made shell,
A civilized shell,
A tin can.
Her broad decks low
Waves nosing scuppers,
Her holds full,
Her decks piled high
With green lumber
From the Carolinas.

Always under sail
With a sweet bilge
And a salt breeze.

Chesapeake in summertime,
Morning southwest breeze,
The midday calm,
And quiet evening harbors
Where the peepers sing.
Following the rockfish,
The blue fish, the hard crab,
Trimming her sails
With the gulls' wings.
Chesapeake when autumn comes,
A million buckets of blue bay
Could never quench the blaze
Of bright fall woods afire
With colors rampant,
While overhead great geese
Call loud for her to follow
And flights of canvasback
Match her great wings.
Winter comes to Chesapeake,
Black ice at Solomons,
No lap of waves to
Match the winter wind
Whining through her rigging.

Long hours around the stove,
Seven-up with a greasy deck,

Waiting for a spring
That soon must come.
Chesapeake in May,
She rests on the ways,
New paint and hemp,
While shores turn bright
With fresh delight,
And with the dogwood
Comes spring snow.

For years she sailed
This inland sea,
And lived to work,
To rest and dream
Of larger cargoes,
Sweeter cargoes,
And a crew
Who loved a breeze.
Then came the wheels,
Paddle wheels,
Hoarse voices of steamers
In tune with night
And windless fog.
Ship wheels,
Runty freight boats,
Turning twin screws,
Turning men's hearts
Away from the wind.
Truck wheels,
A ten ton Mack,
A trailer of beans,

With Sadie's diner
And slot machines.
Wind or wheels,
Wind or wheels,
Wind or wheels,
And the wheels won.

Fewer cargoes, smaller cargoes,
Patched sails and a leaky boat,
Old rope and cheap paint,
Canned beans and a banker's note.
Soon came the choice,
Despoil her,
Tear down her sails,
Rip out her masts,
Her painted bowsprit,
Put an engine in,
Make her a runty freighter
With a scummy bilge
And a slobbering wake,
Or beach her.

There she lies,
They say one day
She made twelve knots,
Coming up the bay.
Why downcast eyes?
She'll sail again
When the fullest moon
Shall rise.

About These Stories

Gilbert Byron was known as "the Thoreau of the Chesapeake" and "the Voice of the Chesapeake." We first came across his work in the basement of the cozy and quaint Old Fox Books and Coffeehouse in Annapolis, Maryland. His book *The Lord's Oysters* is a staple on the Chesapeake's local literature shelves, a somewhat autobiographical fiction depicting the boyhood escapades of a Chesapeake waterman's son. While it provides a good flavor of life on the Eastern Shore, the book contains language we find problematic today and racist themes characteristic of his era. "The Fullest Moon," from a collection of his poetry, instead depicts the quintessential Eastern Shore landscape from which he comes, and the boats that dot its landscape.

Born in Chestertown, Maryland, in 1903, the same month and day as Henry David Thoreau, Byron wrote extensively for more than fifty years, capturing aspects of the Chesapeake's tidewaters that are vanishing with time. He taught high school English and lived in a small cabin on the banks of the Old House Cove off San Domingo Creek near St. Michaels, Maryland, where he wrote numerous poems, books, articles, and essays. The cabin was moved to Pickering Creek Audubon Center in Easton, Maryland, where visitors can go on a self-guided tour and find its walls now adorned by poems inspired by Byron's writing.

Ghost Fleet of Mallows Bay

DONALD G. SHOMETTE

Excerpt from *Ghost Fleet of Mallows Bay:*
And Other Tales of the Lost Chesapeake

It was a frosty, brisk morning when we shoved off into the open Potomac from the dock at General Smallwood State Park on Mattawoman Creek.

The candied colors of early autumn were splashed in bright, irregular patterns along the shore, and the October sky was cloudless, marred only by the vapor trail of a jet flying somewhere near the edge of its earthly envelope. For a day so perfect, however, the river appeared devoid of its usual boaters. With the singular exception of a young whitetailed deer swimming across the creek from the appropriately named Deer Point, nothing seemed to stir. It was perhaps fitting that all signs of human activity had seemingly disappeared from the scene, for our objective was a place of a somewhat peculiar, indeed, unique nature. By the map, we were bound for an obscure, marshy indent on the Maryland shore, a forgotten alcove of time inhabited only by creatures of fur, fin, and feather, and the vestigial remnants of a maritime era long dead.

Upon entering the main channel, Pete Petrone of *National Geographic*, my father, Grady Shomette, and I were instantly struck with the wide majesty of this most historic of American rivers. Between our point of embarkation and our ultimate destination, only a few miles along on the watery highway from the nation's capital, many pivotal events of American history had taken place. Here, in 1608, the indomitable Captain John Smith had explored, searched for precious metals, and gauged the measure of the native inhabitants. Here, shiploads of colonists had landed to challenge and then push back the Tidewater frontier, founding hamlets, towns, and cities as they went. Here, Loyalists and Patriots had engaged in bloody riverine warfare during the Revolutionary War, and British invaders, hell-bent on the capture of the city of Alexandria during the War of 1812, had arrived to chastise President "Jemmy" Madison for daring to declare war on the mightiest seapower in the world. And here, between Mattawoman Creek and Liverpool Point, tens of thousands of Union troops had fortified the coastline to counter a feared Confederate invasion of Maryland during the early days of the Civil War. . . .

As we passed closely along the sandy cliffs of Stump Neck and neared the mouth of Chickamuxen Creek, the rusted bones of a retired and decaying U.S. Navy assault craft, perhaps a veteran of a more recent conflict, lay hard against the shore. Her machine gun turrets were empty and her once-strong back appeared broken, a rusting memento of the more sinister side of civilization. Soon, the shallow cliffs of Moss Point, once known as Budd's Ferry, and the shoally indent of Goose Creek, both sites of Union waterfront batteries and breastworks, were far behind us. Only the giant, modern web of power lines sweeping across the river from the power station above Quantico Creek spoiled the pristine panorama.

The visible evidence of the sprawling U.S. Marine Corps Base at Quantico seemed but a defect on the far horizon. A few miles ahead of us was the modest protrusion known as Sandy Point, on the northern perimeter of our area of investigation. Beached on the shores of the point, and all but hidden from view by the forest that was gradually enveloping it, lay a giant, silent guardian, the skeletal remains of a once-great ship.

As we approached the point, the wreck was invisible against the brilliantly colored backdrop of autumnal foliage. Full-sized trees had grown from its heart, and underbrush camouflaged its waist. A sand spit had grown up around its starboard side as vessel and earth had gradually begun to merge into one after decades of unremitting action by wind, waves, and tides. I dubbed the ancient ship "The Sentinel Wreck." Soon, we bumped ashore and began to explore the great old wooden hulk and the thickly covered terrain surrounding her. I was intrigued by the degree of structural integrity remaining despite the ongoing natural integration process even now under way. Iron pins which had once held its planks in place still stood in orderly rows, beneath canopies of pretty pink wildflowers and brush, as if awaiting marching orders. The area was, indeed, lush with life: evidence of myriad insects, birds, fish, and even deer, raccoon, and otter was everywhere. A great blue heron, flushed from his cover by our arrival, lifted majestically off the stern of the wreck, leaving his half eaten meal behind. Nearby, in the thick underbrush, the remains of a large wooden ship's bulkhead lay adjacent to a pile of weathered vine-covered ship timbers. The Sentinel Wreck, it appeared, had been abandoned while in the very process of being broken up. To the immediate south of the hulk, near the ruins of an ancient wharf, lay the bones of yet another victim of time, a massive wooden barge, hauled up for the last time on the debris-strewn beach an eon before us.

Our destination was an obscure mile-long indent in the Charles County, Maryland, shore fed by a pair of even more obscure streams. As we rounded the northern lip of the embayment, the full and stunning scope of its unique contents was suddenly revealed to us. For almost as far as we could see, masked by the green mantle of nature, lay the greatest assemblage of historic shipwrecks in one discrete location in all of America, more than one hundred vessels dating from the period of the American Revolution to the Space Age. Here, in a place that time had forgotten, slept the Ghost Fleet of Mallows Bay.

It is a minor geographic feature on the big map of the Potomac River drainage system, this little indent of shoreline known as Mallows Bay. Surrounded by low bluffs of up to fifty feet in elevation that frequently meet the water's edge, it lies more than thirty miles south of Washington, D.C., and sixty-five miles from the Chesapeake. The heavily wooded highlands surrounding its narrow beaches between Sandy Point on the north and Liverpool Point on the south are here and there gouged and sliced by ravines of some depth. Two short, meandering creeks, Liverpool and Marlow's, feed into the river near its southern end and drain substantial and scenic wetlands. It is a shallow embayment, situated directly on the salt water–fresh water interface of the river and as such is a natural spawning ground, nursery, and habitat for anadromous and semi-anadromous fishes. Its bottom consists of soft muds and silts in which myriad forms of microscopic life thrive. And its beaches, shores, and forested bluffs, like much of

Charles County, host animals of innumerable varieties, from the majestic American bald eagle, osprey, and egret to the playful river otter, beaver, and painted tortoise. As they say, biodiversity at its finest. It was not always so. And its history? Well, let's just say it's checkered with a different form of diversity. . . .

As our boat pressed into the heart of Mallows Bay on that sunny October day, Pete Petrone, my father, and I spoke almost in hushed tones, as if we had entered some hallowed sanctorum. From the main river channel, the graveyard of ships was barely decipherable, for the bones of many of these long forgotten hulks, several disguised by a necklace of vegetation and a crown of trees, barely pierced the surface of the still waters within, and were visible in outline form only. Most were indistinguishable from the backdrop of forest that crowded the elevated shoreline. The wrecks at the northern end of the embayment over time had filled with collapsed wooden hull siding, sediments, fire charred timbers, rotting vegetation, and more than half a century's worth of Potomac River flotsam and jetsam, creating incredibly rich soils. In the process, they had evolved into islands, some with mini-forests up to twenty-five feet or more in height growing from their hearts, and so tightly crammed with foliage that boarding was all but impossible. A few had floated ashore or had been pulled up, bow first, hard against the beach, while the noses of others, with rusted steel cables dipping off at odd angles into the water, actually abutted the sides of steep bluffs. And everywhere, there was life, radiant, and in utter profusion.

The waters within the bay were now clotted with thick mats of hydrilla, a Eurasian plant that had been introduced to the Potomac in the mid-1980s to help clean up pollution. It fouled our prop, obscured from view the thousands of obstructions lying just below the surface, and forced us to conduct our explorations under oars alone. White feathered sentinels watched our every motion with spectral eyes from their perch on a line of three score of pilings, marking the southern perimeter of the bay. All about us, untold numbers of ships lay in varying states of decomposition. Many were festooned with the leafy burnished colors of autumn, while others revealed only the wicked crossed teeth of iron strapping that once reinforced wooden hulls long since burned or rotted away. As we passed beyond the piling line, more hulks lay just beneath the waters, adjacent to a giant steel-hulled ship. The great vessel, which appeared to be a relatively recent arrival, apparently had been abandoned while in the very process of being dismantled and pinned to the bay floor by immense piles of cement blocks dumped on her stern. . . .

· + ·

As we continued to explore the intriguing nooks and crannies of this lost corner of history, I thought back to my first visit to the embayment thirty years before, and then to my last, in 1963, as an art student in college. I was by then too old for ghosts, and there were more practical things to occupy a young man's interests. I had come to shoot footage for a short clip for my film production class at Pratt Institute, in Brooklyn, New York, on a subject I was certain would not be duplicated by my fellow students—the Ghost Fleet of Mallows Bay. But in the process, I began to realize, even then, that the bay was changing dramatically. The ship remains were slowly, but perceptibly, being altered as plant and tree roots gouged ever more deeply into the matrix of their old hulls. The still waters of the bay were, in those days, covered by the telltale signs of a river struggling to stay alive. A foul-smelling soup of pea green algae, perhaps a half inch thick, swirled slowly about the surface. The bloated odoriferous bodies of dead fish clustered in every hollow of the bay, lapped by thick, dirty waters of almost molasses-like consistency. The newspapers, during those early years of environmental consciousness, had been filled with accounts of the dramatic increase in river pollution and the life forms that were disappearing because of it.

Yet nature was fighting back. Here and there, as if to punctuate the fact, a great blue heron would rise up, incensed at our intrusion, and escape to a more remote sector of the basin. The wrecks themselves, some even then brimming with growth, seemed to be coming to life despite the poisonous waters of the Potomac. The abandoned hulks were being changed by a strange and wondrous metamorphosis which saw the discarded, wasted products of an industrial society slowly transform into many thriving micro-environments.

The mystery of Mallows Bay was still there, albeit more mired in the black, muddy bottom with every passing year. Just who had built these great ships and why? Why were they here, in this forsaken, albeit beautiful, setting so close to, but isolated from, the civilized world? My father, for me the fount of all wisdom, had no answers. I vowed that day that I would find out....

From high altitude, the shipwrecks of Mallows Bay look, for all the world, like a vast fleet of warships lying at anchor in a snug harbor awaiting orders to sail. Yet, as we were soon to discover, the Mallows Bay transect and all of the ships and features within it were, in reality, an enormous jigsaw puzzle that at times appeared to us so intricate that it might never be reassembled. A single change of tide, which could cover a third of the fleet from view in an hour, made navigation amidst the labyrinthine lanes between hulks, which was never easy, frequently impossible. From late June through early October, hydrilla strangled the bay and everything in it. The still waters of Mallows Bay were now often so densely choked that even a canoe passed only with difficulty, and diving operations were carried out at some hazard. . . .

· ✦ ·

Exploration and surveying onboard a wooden steamship hull, filled with waist-deep water and frequently populated by snapping turtles, water snakes, and fish and covered by slimy hydrilla which often obscured all surface visibility of the bottom, was something less than an adventure. Even the tiny minnows, ever eager to feed on a bit of peeling sunburned skin, were a nuisance. Adding to these minor difficulties were the distinct hazards caused by thousands of iron pins, fittings, and sharp, broken timbers sticking up from the decks, each of which was capable of tearing a hole through one's foot, wet suit boot and all—and frequently did! Onboard the dry hulks covered by almost impenetrable vegetation, snakes were regularly encountered but proved far less of a vexation than the black flies, mosquitoes, spiders, ticks, and the thousand-and-one other insects that can make life miserable in a jungle-like environment on a 95-degree summer day in the open sun. Of course, attempting to survey hulks in freezing water along the unprotected outer line, directly exposed to the waves and currents of the Potomac on a cold, windy day in March, while struggling to keep from being washed out to sea, was no picnic either. At such moments, . . . it was often tempting to chuck the whole thing. But then some new discovery would make it all worthwhile—until the next unforeseen difficulty. . . .

· ✦ ·

[It] was our last survey target that was to be the most visually dramatic—an intact shipwreck that lay at the southern terminus of the transect. Immediately below the piling stubs of the old Liverpool Point steamboat wharf, drawn up with her bow ashore and her stern in eight feet of water, lies the sad ruins of the North Carolina Atlantic menhaden fishing boat *Mermentau*.

Mementau presents the classic picture of a fatally stranded ship, with her distinctive, graceful hull tilted to one side on the beach and her white pilot house torn askew. On her rounded stern, the shadow outline of her name can be traced in the darks and lights of the wood. Although her single mast still stands and her aft cabins are intact, she is a sad sight. Built in 1949 at Beaufort, North Carolina, for the Gulf Menhaden Company, she was 199 tons gross, 153 tons net, 121.7 feet in length, 20.6 feet abeam, and 9.8 feet deep in hold. She was an oil screw ship, with engines capable of producing 400 horsepower. . . .

Now, she was occupied by beavers and river otters who had taken up residence in her hold, and by a family of osprey living in her crow's nest.

Upon boarding the ship and looking northward toward Mallows Bay, Sandy Point, and beyond, I was struck with all we have seen and discovered within the space of less than a few miles and a few months. Here, in the wrecks and ruins of a century, perhaps two, lay an enormous concentration of the physical remains of a pivotal, defining moment in American history, a vast repository of American maritime design and technology sleeping serenely in the environment for which it was intended. We had explored, mapped, and studied the remains of probably the largest shipwreck assemblage in the nation, and possibly the world. We had seen and documented the physical evidence of mankind's genius, stupidity, intellect, avarice, drive, ignorance, and waste. We had plumbed the depths of a fourteen-year-old's fantasy, and we had barely scratched the surface.

About This Story

Marine archaeologist and historian Donald Shomette first saw the ghost ships in the Potomac River's Mallows Bay when he was on a camping trip as a teenager. Over the years he came back time and again, and eventually he and his research team came to know this bay and its ships intimately, surveying and creating an exhaustive archaeological record. As he documents in his book *The Ghost Fleet of Mallows Bay,* here the remains of what is possibly the largest shipwreck fleet in the world are being reclaimed by nature, and the ships are perhaps becoming more useful as habitat than they were in their original incarnation. In fact, many of these ships never sailed.

Most of the ships in the Ghost Fleet were built in response to President Woodrow Wilson's national call to arms in 1917 in anticipation of warfare with Germany. Wooden warships were cheaper and quicker to build than steel ships, which was extra important as Germany's submarines were sinking ships faster than they could be built. Political opposition and bureaucracy delayed the production of these ships, and the Germans surrendered in 1918 before the fleet was complete. Of the nearly three hundred that had been built by 1920, many were leaky, poorly constructed, and too small for long-distance cargo hauling. Since the shift to diesel power made these coal-burning ships obsolete and they were expensive to keep afloat, most of the ships were ultimately sold for salvage, then burned over a period of dozens of years and sunk into the muddy bay floor.

Decades later the wrecks had become such a vital part of the marine ecosystem that removing them would create more pollution and harm to the environment than keeping them in place. Shomette writes, "The shipwrecks of Mallows Bay have created a synthetic environment that, in its slow but certain evolution, has held and enriched the sediments. This environment seemingly counteracts the pollution of the Potomac's water, filtering it and providing habitat and food to a wide range of life forms. In the process, each vessel has become a mini-ecosystem. Just as it was once the last refuge of the Potomac snowy egret and the site of Maryland's last sturgeon fishery, so Mallows Bay has again blossomed with biodiversity. In many ways it is like a giant artificial reef to which the creatures of the sea and air flock to flourish, reclaiming this stretch of the river once and for all from the trauma of the industrial age."

In 2019, this 18-square-mile stretch of the Potomac River was designated the Mallows Bay–Potomac River National Marine Sanctuary—the first national marine sanctuary within the Chesapeake Bay watershed—protecting its resting ships and the abundant life it has become home to. This sanctuary provides recreational access and incredible wildlife viewing for walkers and paddlers, while also preserving the Bay's cultural heritage and history related to its ships and the Piscataway people native to this land.

Harriet Tubman, Woodswoman

TIYA MILES

Adapted from *Night Flyer: Harriet Tubman*
and the Faith Dreams of a Free People

Harriet Tubman, the dauntless Underground Railroad activist of the nineteenth century, is one of the most widely recognized women in United States history. Following her bold escape from slavery on the Eastern Shore of the Chesapeake Bay in Maryland, Tubman returned to the South to guide approximately seventy individuals to freedom in the US North and Canada. During the Civil War, she joined in a military campaign known as the Combahee River Raid, which freed more than seven hundred people from South Carolina rice plantations. Statues and plaques have been erected in Tubman's honor, and she is, according to a national survey cited by the historian Lois Horton, "among the top ten most famous people in American history."[1] The state of Maryland established a crowning public commemoration of Tubman's achievements in the form of the Harriet Tubman Underground Railroad State Park in 2007 and later the Harriet Tubman Underground Railroad Visitor Center on its grounds in

2017, a learning center integrated into the natural surroundings abutting the Blackwater National Wildlife Refuge.

Tubman's most graceful memorial, though, grows directly from the ground. In the early 1900s, in Auburn, New York, members of her family planted a testament in her honor. Judith Bryant, a great-grand-niece of Tubman, said: "The children . . . planted a small tree in Fort Hill. They thought it was a small Christmas tree and would stay forever small. And it is now the tallest tree in the cemetery. It's a Norway Spruce, and it is the landmark for the grave of Harriet Tubman."[2] An evergreen tree is a fitting symbol of Tubman's life. From her adolescent years in Maryland, she gravitated toward trees, cultivating a knowledge of forestlands. As the environmental sociologist Dorceta Taylor has noted, Tubman "reveled in solitude and used it as a space for contemplation when she was alone in the woods."[3] Tubman's affinity with forests made her own escape from slavery and her lauded Underground Railroad rescues possible.

Harriet Tubman was born Araminta "Minty" Ross to enslaved parents Rit Green and Ben Ross, around 1822. After she married, Araminta Ross would change her name, taking on her mother's first name, Harriet, and her husband's last name, Tubman. As a child, Tubman faced severe neglect as well as physical and emotional abuse as her owner (who also owned Tubman's mother and the other Green-Ross children) leased her out to others. From around the age of six, Tubman was living away from her mother and performing arduous outdoor work for various enslavers who would pay her owner. She became ill during these extreme circumstances of forced labor and was repeatedly sent back home, where she was nursed back to health by her mother. On one occasion when Tubman was a teen, she was severely injured. An overseer threw a heavy weight that hit her in the head, causing lasting cognitive effects that included seizures, headaches, and visions.

Following this head injury, Tubman found herself hired out to John Stewart, "a man for the heaviest kind of out-of-door labor," according to Emma Telford, who knew Tubman in New York after her escape. Tubman's task list went beyond the grueling yet customary field work that Black women were often assigned. As a teenage girl, Tubman "drove oxen, carted, ploughed, cut wood and hauled logs, performing Herculean tasks," Telford recorded.[4] Another contemporary of Tubman's in the North, Sarah Bradford, wrote. "The labor of the horse and the ox, the lifting of barrels and flour and other heavy weights were given to her."[5] Tubman carried out this masculinized type of work in 1830s Maryland, a place of diverse demographics and labor routines that were multiplying as she matured into young womanhood.

Tubman toiled like this for five years, also carrying the silent burden of a disability. She continued to suffer from seizures and pounding headaches, and she would lose consciousness during conversations or in the middle of physical tasks. During years of hard physical exertion performed through the fog of chronic pain while she was still enslaved, Tubman feared the future. "I was not happy or contented," she later told a reporter in Canada. "[E]very time I saw a white man I was afraid of being carried away. I had two sisters carried away in a chain-gang; one of them left two children. We were always uneasy."[6]

It was during these challenging years that Tubman requested permission to organize her own time and earnings by hiring herself out. She would gain greater autonomy and the chance to earn cash, while her owner would benefit by ridding himself of the hassle of managing her leases. Now she completed her labor on terms that she had negotiated with Stewart, whose operation included two-hundred-plus acres of plantation land and hundreds of forested land, as well as mercantile, lumber, and shipbuilding businesses.[7] Tubman expanded her knowledge of various industries as she listened in on exchanges among Stewart, his employees, his customers, and those he enslaved, broadening her mental map of the region in a way that would prove consequential years later when she escaped.

Tubman's tasks took her to the wooded areas of Stewart's acreage where workers, paid and unpaid, had been assigned to dig a canal for the transport of logs and other valuable materials. The work was physically demanding but also exhilarating. Out in the woods, she could feel more free. "She loved the beauty; she loved the quiet [in Maryland]," said the current director of the Harriet Tubman Home in New York, Karen Hill.[8] At the same time, Tubman realized that the natural world she loved was also the scene of her exploitation. She was forced to labor for others here because the land, also a victim, could produce profit for her enslavers. Knowing this, she abided with nature like other enslaved African Americans did—in dual modes of grim recognition and abundant joy. Tubman felt an emotional affinity with natural things and may have experienced time outdoors as a balm.

The work in nature may have eased the toll of her disability, too. Ednah Cheney, who knew Tubman later in life, wrote: "The blow produced a disease of the brain which was severe for a long time, and still makes her very lethargic. She cannot remain quiet fifteen minutes without appearing to fall asleep. It is not refreshing slumber; but a heavy, weary condition which exhausts her. She therefore loves great physical activity, and direct heat of the sun, which keeps her blood actively circulating."[9] During these teenage years, Tubman "learned to love the land, where flora and wildlife reflected seasonal change," the historian Catherine Clinton has written.[10] This love of the land would expand and take on new dimensions as outdoor work led her into reunion with her father, Ben Ross. The adolescent Araminta Ross—soon to become Harriet Tubman—was becoming a woodswoman.

Ben Ross, an experienced lumberjack, gained his freedom sometime in the 1830s and took a job with John Stewart, his enslaved daughter's employer.[11] Tubman, still a teenager, began to work in the woods as a member of her father's crew, the only female among the men. Sarah Bradford wrote of this period: "Frequently she worked with her father, who was a timber Inspector, and superintended the cutting and hauling of great quantities of timber for the Baltimore ship-yards. . . . While engaged with her father, she would cut wood, haul logs, etc."[12] As she worked, Tubman absorbed new information about trees, plants, weather, and animal behavior while honing her skills in reading landscapes as well as people. She saw her father lead small groups through thick mud beneath dense tree canopy, managing them in the pursuit of a common purpose. "That landscape became her classroom," the historian Kate Larson has said. "She learned how to survive in those woods. She learned how to read the night sky."[13] As Dorceta Taylor has noted: "Her father also taught her how to move silently through the forest, imitate bird calls, and use bird sounds to communicate with others. He also taught her how to feel the barks of trees for moss—the moss grew more heavily on the north side of the trees and thus pointed the way north."[14]

Tubman saw this period of her life as foundational. In retrospect, she would describe this critical time as preparatory and even providential. "I was getting fitted for the work the Lord was getting ready for me," she said.[15] Less than a decade later, as she wended her way to freedom in 1849 and then aided scores of people in their escapes, Tubman would read the trees, subsist on plants, and imitate the barred owl's call as an all-clear sign.[16] As she matured from adolescence into young womanhood, Harriet Tubman learned much from her father. Surely, she had other teachers, too, in the methods of outdoor survival. Tubman was not a lone heroic figure but rather someone embedded in social as well as ecological networks.

Harriet Tubman's liberation mission unfolded in living natural contexts—upon and among the lands and waters of the Chesapeake Bay. Tubman observed, understood, and accessed features of her environment, often enlisting them in her freedom crusade. And more than that, her "repeated journeys into slaveholding America" required "ecological confidence," in the words of the environmental studies scholar Kimberly Ruffin.[17] Tubman studied the elements of nature around her, connecting with plants, trees, animals, and stars, until she became, as Angela Crenshaw, current acting superintendent of Maryland State Parks, has put it, "the ultimate outdoors woman."[18]

Just as Tubman learned from her family and community, we can learn from Tubman's relationship with nature. Shock and deep adaptation may lie ahead. But climate activists can be inspired by the ultimate outdoors woman's model of hope and resilience.

About This Story

The Harriet Tubman Underground Railroad State Park is a 17-acre site on the Harriet Tubman Underground Railroad Byway, which leads drivers to various heritage sites throughout the region. The visitor center, which opened in 2017, features exhibits about her life in the Choptank River region and beyond, celebrating her bravery, courage, and lasting legacy. It was here that we learned how Harriet used her knowledge of the stars and the Chesapeake landscape to navigate the Underground Railroad escape routes, and here that we became interested in Harriet's story as a naturalist.

We reached out to Tiya Miles, Michael Garvey Professor of History at Harvard University, a 2011 MacArthur fellow, and author of seven books, including including *Wild Girls: How the Outdoors Shaped the Women Who Challenged a Nation* and other prize-winning histories of American slavery. Her response could not have thrilled us more, as she was just completing *Night Flyer: Harriet Tubman and the Faith Dreams of a Free People*, a book on Harriet Tubman's environmental sensibility, and she offered to create an essay adapted from the new book. The essay reveals aspects of Harriet's life and legacy that were new to us and offers inspiration and a sense of hope to climate activists, from a place where climate and history weigh heavy.

Creation of Toolup Ahkiy

NANTICOKE INDIAN TRIBE
as told by RAGGHIRAIN

Kiisheelumukweengw, the "One who creates through thought," thought the world into being.

There came a time very long ago but not so long ago that we have forgotten. The animals lived in deep Nip (Water), but not too deep, with no dry Kikun Ahkiyii (Earth Mother). They grew weary of being wet and wanted to find a way to bring up the mud from under the Nip (Water) to create dry Kikun Ahkiyii (Earth Mother).

All the animals, from the biggest to the almost smallest, dived into the Nip (Water) in one swift motion. One by one, they tried to dive deep enough to bring up some of the mud.

One by one, they failed, unable to dive deep enough and hold their breath long enough under the Nip (Water). It seemed as though not one could bring up the muddy Kikun Ahkiyii (Earth Mother) from the bottom.

No one was willing to risk their lives, so they returned to the surface, gasping for air. It seemed impossible. And no one was ready to give up their lives to bring up the muddy Kikun Ahkiyii (Earth Mother).

Finally, after all the others had tried and failed, the smallest among them, Wiihkee (Muskrat), wanted to try, but everyone laughed at Wiihkee (Muskrat). "You are too small, silliness."

Once again, they started laughing. Wiihkee (Muskrat) slipped away from all her relatives, splashed into the deepest part of the Nip (Water), and took her turn. Everyone turned when they heard the splash and began to call out "No! No! Wiihkee (Muskrat), it's too dangerous; please come back."

Wiihkee (Muskrat) dove deeper and deeper under the Nip (Water). The other animals feared Wiihkee (Muskrat) would lose her life, for she stayed below the Nip (Water) much longer than any of the other animals had remained under the Nip (Water).

All the relatives were worried and searched in the Nip (Water) for Wiihkee (Muskrat) but could not find her. When Wiihkee (Muskrat) finally emerged to the surface, she was on the brink of death, completely exhausted.

They gathered Wiihkee (Muskrat) into their paws and spotted a cluster of perhaps Kikun Ahkiyii (Earth Mother) Wiihkee (Muskrat) had scratched from the very bottom of the surface of the deepest part of Nip (Water). Wiihkee (Muskrat) held what she had found tightly in her paw.

Kiisheelumukweengw, the "One who creates through thought," had been watching all that was going on and called Toolup (Turtle) to the surface of the Nip (Water) and placed the mud from Wiihkee's (Muskrat's) paw upon the back of Toolup (Turtle).

Kiisheelumukweengw, the "One who creates through thought," caused the Kikun Ahkiyii (Earth Mother) to grow, covering Toolup's (Turtle's) back. As Toolup (Turtle) continued to rise, she grew larger and larger. Her back drained off the Nip (Water), and the Ahkiy (Earth) expanded and grew, then began to dry, becoming Toolup Ahkiy (Turtle Island).

All of Our Relatives live upon this new dry Kikun Ahkiyii (Earth Mother).

One day, in the middle of the Kikun Ahkiyii (Earth Mother), a Cedar tree grew upon the back of Toolup Ahkiy (Turtle Island). From the Cedar tree grew a shoot, which eventually sprouted, and out stepped Ahkwaahaak (the first woman).

Ahkwaahaak (the first woman) enjoyed living among her relatives but still hoped for one like herself. The tree grew a second shoot, and Naap (man) sprouted. Ahkwaahaak (the first woman) was surprised because this one was not like her. After a while, they became friends.

Ahkwaahaak and Naap are our Ancestors who came before us, and we are their Descendants. Our elders have told us that this is truth.

Wiihkee (Muskrat), though small in stature, had a great heart for her relatives. She was prepared to sacrifice everything, even her own life, for the sake of her community. She embodies the time-honored customs of our Tribal Society and of those who give selflessly of themselves. With loving care to create and nurture the bounty of Turtle Island. Waanishii Wiihkee.

Kiisheelumukweengw *key-shall-ah-MOW-kwang* (Creator / "One who creates through thought")
Nip (Water)
Kikun Ahkiyii *kick-UN AH*key-e* (Earth Mother)
Wiihkee *wee-h'-kay* (Muskrat)

Toolup *TOLL-up* (Turtle)
Ahkiy *uh*-KEY* (Earth)
Toolup Ahkiy (Turtle Island)
Ahkwaahaak *ah*-KWA-hawk* (the first woman)
Naap *nahp* (man)

About This Story

The Nanticoke ("People of the Tidewater") lived along the Kuskarawaok (now Nanticoke) River. They were among the largest tribes along the Eastern Shore, allied with the Powhatan Confederacy, when Europeans first arrived in the area.

On their website, the tribe shares this story of their first encounter with Captain John Smith in 1608:

> *While exploring the Chesapeake Bay, Smith and his crew sailed onto the Kuskarawaok River. The Kuskarawaoks, later known as the Nanticoke Indians, cautiously watched Smith's ship from the shore, climbing into the trees for a better look. When Smith approached the shore in a boat, the Nanticoke answered with arrows. Smith prudently put down anchor for the night in the middle of the river. The next morning, the Nanticoke appeared on the shore with baskets of food. Still cautious, Captain Smith had his men fire muskets over the heads of the Nanticoke. Later that afternoon, Smith noticed the Indians were gone, and he and his men came to shore. He found fires still burning, but no Indians were seen. Smith discovered glass beads, shells, and copper pieces left as gifts of friendship. The following day, four Indians who had been fishing approached Smith's ship in a canoe. Smith convinced them he came in friendship, and they returned with*

twenty villagers. Food, water, and furs were exchanged for gifts the English brought . . . Smith described the Nanticoke as "the best merchants of all."

Over the years that followed, however, European settlers seized Nanticoke land and forced tribes out of their villages. An eighteenth century proposal set aside thousands of acres of land for a Nanticoke reservation, but the stipulations limited their ability to leave for seasonal hunting, and conflicts with traders and settlers continued. Many of the Nanticoke chose to leave, accepting an offer to join the Six Nations of the Iroquois in New York, Pennsylvania, and Canada. Others moved west, seeking more territory. Those who remained on the Eastern Shore assimilated and purchased land. They became recognized as a legal entity by the state of Delaware in 1881 and acquired tribally owned lands and property.

Today, the Nanticoke Indian Museum preserves their stories. The only Native American museum in the state of Delaware, the space collects and displays items that explore the heritage of tide-water tribes, and organizes cultural events traditions like an annual powwow, which brings together tribes from all along the East Coast. While we were researching for this book, the museum connected us with Raggatha "RagghiRain," a Tsalagi descendant and the one of many storytellers who share legends that have been passed down through generations.

In addition to sharing stories, RagghiRain introduced us to Tidewater Park in Laurel, Delaware, where the stories she tells come to life. The park's name is translated from the Algonquin word Nanticoke, meaning "people of the Tidewater." Visitors to the park and playground can encounter a giant turtle, a squirrel, a wooden beaver, and a rainbow crow—animals that appear in Nanticoke legends—in ways meant to incorporate play with learning while preserving Nanticoke culture. Accompanying plaques and QR codes tell the stories to park visitors, directly from a traditional storyteller.

As someone who follows traditional teachings, RagghiRain often does not sign her name to the stories she tells. One should not elevate oneself, she told us. But for *Campfire Stories*, thinking of her children and grandchildren, and with the support of the Chief of the Nanticoke, as well as a Council member, RagghiRain agreed to be credited as the storyteller for this section. To the readers of Campfire Stories, RagghiRain notes the following:

> *We do not choose to be the Keeper of the Living Stories.*
> *We were chosen before we could speak.*
> *Yet it is our choice to travel this Sacred Walk for the Seven Generations.*
> *Speaking Truth through Stories, do not see us; hear the truth within the stories, allowing the seeds to grow within your spirit.*
> *May we all plant seeds of truth and healing.*

Skipjack

CHRISTOPHER WHITE

Excerpt from *Skipjack: The Story of*
America's Last Sailing Oystermen

ome late March along the Chesapeake, winter often lingers, reluctant to let go. The pattern is familiar: A nor' wester shuttles in a cold front from the Canadian plains and thoughts of spring are pirated off to sea. The night air drops to freezing, rebounding just a fraction perhaps into the low forties—by noon the next day. The sun climbs high and the wind lessens. But the Bay itself remains frigid. Its waters are slow to revive; they stay wintry till May. Only then will hibernating crabs emerge from their muddy repose. Yes, four or five weeks till any market, the locals say. Oyster dredging is over, and the crabs haven't started to crawl. In the idiom of the Chesapeake, it's "slack time." Slack season, especially when the weather is raw.

On one of those cold, slack nights—neither winter nor spring—I drove a little too fast down Route 33 on Maryland's Eastern Shore, the left bank of the Chesapeake, toward Tilghman Island, to board the skipjack *Rebecca T. Ruark* before she left port. Built in 1886, she was among the last sailboats still employed in commercial fishing in North America. Only nineteen of her sister skipjacks remained. The wind-powered fleet had just completed another season dredging oysters from the bottom of the Bay—by sail, the only legal way to dredge for these shellfish in Maryland, most of the week. To some an anachronism, to others a symbol of sustainability, skipjacks had been dredging on the Bay since the 1880s, and I had always wanted to see one up close—before they disappeared.

But my mind was elsewhere. The LED numbers on the car's digital clock warned: 3:10. *Rebecca* would depart the dock in twenty minutes. I was running late.

The evening before, on the phone, Captain Wade Murphy had said I should arrive at the wharf by three thirty. "We'll eat breakfast on the way to the oyster beds," he had said, startling me. I had actually blinked. The first time you hear "three thirty" from a "waterman"—the Chesapeake name for a fisherman—you figure he must be talking about the afternoon. But he isn't. Murphy said to get a good night's sleep; tomorrow would be a long day. . . .

"Ain't drudging again 'til November," he had said at the meeting. "But right now we're planting seed for harvest in two or three years. If ya'd like to go spatting one day, ye're welcome to it. Just don't be late." Watermen are known for being punctual—it is an obsession, though nothing else in their lives is kept up to date. As keepers of an ancient art, they abide by a different calendar.

At this, their most crucial moment in history—the likely crash of the oyster—the majority of watermen stuck to their old ways: independent, stubborn, distrustful of others. Thus, for two weeks I had been talking to scientists and resource managers, getting only half the story. Oysters, like other Chesapeake fisheries, had peaked years ago (15 million bushels in 1884), and more recently—after years in the 2-million-bushel range—had plummeted, dipping below 200,000 bushels in 1996. Formerly the nation's largest producer of shellfish, the Chesapeake was no longer king of the American oyster. But what was causing the drop in landings? Overharvesting or mismanagement? Pollution or shellfish disease? The usual suspects. Some environmentalists claimed the fishery would vanish in a couple of years unless a ban on harvesting was imposed. Others said a moratorium wouldn't work. The camps were divided. But I had not yet heard the waterman's view, on his own ground in the middle of the Bay. His opinion would likely be telling. More than the fishery was at stake for the waterman. At stake was his way of life, a lineage for Wade Murphy going back three generations.

So I was quick to accept Murphy's unexpected invitation—to observe oystermen at work. An equal attraction was the chance simply to ride aboard a skipjack, the last in a long line of oyster "dredge boats" that have plied the waters of the Bay. . . .

Tilghman Island—home port to more than half the remaining skipjack fleet lay twenty miles down the road. From the landscape, each mile traveled could have been another ten years regressed into the past. After bypassing the town of Easton and the Black & Decker power tool plant, the road to Tilghman had become more rural and serpentine. Streetlights vanished. Shoulders disappeared. Years peeled away. Under the moonlight, empty fields stretched away from the road like black cloaks. A river appeared to the right—the Miles—and a hump of an old bridge took me over Oak Creek. The car shimmied with a gust of wind.

Up ahead the Victorian architecture of St. Michaels, a former watermen's haunt, loomed into view. Gingerbread houses. Antique stores. Real estate offices. A maritime museum. The residents of St. Michaels no longer lived exclusively off the water. Here Chesapeake workboats were artifacts of history, not the living skipjacks I expected down the road.

I recalculated the distance: twelve miles to go. The clock said: "3:15." Fifteen minutes left. Three small bedroom communities were perched along the hooked peninsula between St. Michaels and Tilghman, a limblike appendage known as Bay Hundred. Gabled homes from the days of schooner captains loomed in the moonlight.

The last five miles to Tilghman Island lasted forever. The clock gave me nine minutes. Watermen houses now lined the highway; crab pots overflowed from pickup trucks onto front lawns. Then, up ahead, I spied the tall masts of the skipjacks across Knapps Narrows, the slim channel dividing Tilghman from the peninsula. The half-dozen, fifty-foot sailboats rose out of the dark water like white ghosts. The drawbridge was down. On it a sign offered FRESH BAIT: EEL AND BULL LIPS and a phone number. Tilghman Island, one of the last authentic watermen villages around.

As I sped across the drawbridge, the iron grates clanked under my tires. Looking left toward the Choptank River, I saw the running lights of a dozen low-lying workboats getting under way. Beyond them, two tall skipjacks were silhouetted in the moonlight near the eastern entrance to the narrows. To my right—west toward the Bay—the treelike masts of four more dredge boats lined the channel, their white sails aloft. My heart raced a little. I had stepped back into the Age of Sail. Like a time traveler, I had entered another world. . . .

· ✦ ·

The wharves resembled a nineteenth-century painting and were brimming with activity. Men, in pairs, lifted baskets onto the boats.

Captains called on their crews to hurry. Hand over hand, men raised sails to dry them out from yesterday's rain. Others ran down the rickety pier, the boards warped and buckled like broken piano keys. The whole entourage moved in concert, with the purpose of a racing crew. The air smelled of brine, and I inhaled it deeply, leaving the window down as I scanned the docks for *Rebecca*. I spotted her southwest of the bridge. . . .

My wristwatch glowed "3:25 A.M." as I crossed the deck of *Sigsbee* and jumped aboard *Rebecca*, spanning three feet of open water, just as the crew cast off the bow line. "Well, it's about time," the captain barked through the dark. He was tall and lanky, like a teenager, and clean-shaven. The rest of his features were obscured by the night. I said good morning to Captain Murphy, noting that I was five minutes early.

   "Heading out a bit arlier than expected," he called out above the slapping of the sails. "Put that gear below. We're having a few problems and ya might learn something." Surrounding me were the tackle and trim of a sailing ship—three-pulley wooden blocks, oak deadeyes, varnished spars, brass fittings, mast hoops—enough nineteenth-century hardware to make an antique dealer swoon. Setting my hand on the cabin top, I discovered it was slick, coated with ice. I regretted leaving cap and gloves in the car. With the wind chill it was well below zero. . . .

Murphy squinted into the dark. "*Nellie Byrd*," he said, meaning Daryl Larrimore, the boy captain, had headed out even earlier than we had "Make it quick, David. I'll be damned if anybody gets to the seed area before me."

David Fluharty, today's first mate, leaned over the stern railing and poured oil into the crankcase of the yawl-boat engine. The yawl boat hung off two steel arms, called "davits," extending beyond the stern like the lifeboats on Titanic. Murphy leaned over and jiggled the battery-cable leads again. They sparked against the night, as if they were shooting stars. Encouraged by that, he reached for the key on the instrument panel. Pop. Pop. Brrrrr. The engine blasted thick smoke into the air and came to life. Captain and first mate unhitched the bow and stern lines that held the yawl boat on the davits and lowered the tender into the water. The yawl boat was now ready to push the skipjack, like a tug. . . .

The captain announced we were heading to Stone Rock, an oyster bed just this side of Sharps Island Light. Oyster beds are regularly called "bars" or "reefs" by scientists. Rarely called reefs by watermen, however, hard-bottom oyster beds are more often referred to as "hard bars" or "rocks." There are hundreds of oyster rocks throughout the Bay and its major rivers. This one, he said, was named for the baseball- to boulder-size stones embedded in the reef. They made dredging difficult, but the state had planted old oyster shells here last summer, around spawning time, in order to host larval oysters, which can swim, as they settled on the reef. The settlers, called seed or spat, attach to the oyster rock. Adult oysters are sedentary, glued to each other or anything that's handy—especially old shells and stones. Both the plantings and spawning had been a success, and the "spat set," the gathering of seed oysters, had yielded a record count. The Stone Rock nursery was the watermen's best hope for a future harvest.

I had to wonder why the oyster was in jeopardy. From the beginning its survival seemed assured, for as early as 1865 the

Maryland legislature passed a law limiting dredging of oysters to sail power. With the potential arrival of steamships, it was one of the earliest conservation statutes in the country. Its continuance has been the equivalent of favoring the horse-drawn plow over the tractor, in what has been termed "enforced obsolescence," to preserve the reefs. Skipjacks are inefficient—that is their saving grace. . . .

In the last minutes of moonlight, two dredge boats passed us by. I asked the captain the name of the skipjack to our right. He cupped his hands around his eyes to shield the moon. Only a dark silhouette glided along the water, mast and sails reaching toward the stars. "*Lady Katie,*" he said. "That's Daryl Larrimore's uncle, Stanley. Thar're only a few drudging families left." Six skipjacks had set sail, nearly a third of the fleet. The remaining captains sat out the spatting season for fear it would cripple their boats, which were already in ill repair. The fleet was in critical condition. After years of braving winter waters, timbers were weak—bone tired. Many skipjacks were unsafe to sail.

"We lose a couple of drudge boats either year," Murphy said, using the vernacular "either" to stand for "every" or "any." "We're down to a dozen or so Tilghman captains and half that at Deal Island farther south. That's only a few boats still living. Even if thar were more captains coming along, the rest of the boats are now dead". . . .

On the voyage south, Murphy turned his attention to the past year's oyster season. "I've been drudging for thirty-nine years," he said, "and last season was the worst year of my life. We've got the little ones; that's not the problem. It's the dying. The dying's been something awful."

The dying off of the oyster population had been underway since the 1960s, after a disease named MSX invaded the Bay's southern, saltier half. Like a blight, it invades a reef, turning live oysters into empty shells. The same disease had wiped out oysters in Delaware Bay and Chincoteague Bay, which are more saline than the Chesapeake and thus more vulnerable. Since then, MSX had crept northward, killing off most of Tangier Sound in the Lower Bay and now threatening the middle Bay and its rivers. Oyster harvests had plummeted at least in part due to the disease. And recent high oyster spawns had not made up the difference. The terrible paradox is that oysters spawn best in saltier water exactly where MSX thrives, Murphy summed up the dilemma: "South of Stone Rock, half the big orsters are dead but the seed looks good. It'll take two or three years for that seed to grow, if it lives or if we move it. Anyway you look at it, it's just gonna take a long time getting the Bay straight." Everywhere predictions for the coming season seemed dire. The watermen would have to fight for every shell. . . .

As we headed south, the gusty wind continued to blow from the northwest at about twenty miles per hour. We were on a "broad reach," the wind off our starboard hindquarter. *Rebecca* moved beautifully, slicing up, over, and through the waves. I had never before sailed at night. With the moon nearly setting, the stars became clearer but offered no warmth. Black sky, black water: only the white skipjack lit up by the moon. In the dark, with the boat prancing and sails billowing, it could have been a night voyage in any one of the past five centuries. Clipper ships. Schooners.

Bugeyes—the local two-masted dredge boat. They had all passed the torch to the skipjack. The moon as witness shone like a spotlight on our sails.

The captain spun the wheel of *Rebecca* to the right, to starboard, to the southwest. Each time Murphy turned his head, the hidden half of his face emerged from the shadows. He pulled in the main sheet a little and sent me forward to do the same to the jib. We were getting close to Stone Rock. In the growing light before dawn, we could see the white workboats gathered in a circle about a mile away. At that distance they looked like whitecaps breaking across the jet-black water.

Finished with the jib sheet, I came back aft. I had been gone only a minute, but, inexplicably, Murphy was furious, red in the face, mad as hell. What had I done?

"Tha're all thar," he spit, pointing into the twilight. "One, two, three, four. Four skipjacks on the rock before sunrise and here I am a mile behind. My crew has been late every day this week. Tommy didn't show up again this morning, so I left him at the dock. I may have to farr his ass". . . .

"That's all I ask—they show up on time," the captain explained. "Once I got them aboard they can't go anywheres. They have to work. All I have to do is encourage them a bit: give them some ambition." Murphy, still flushed, turned back to the wheel. The captain's sudden outbursts were landing too close to my proximity; I vowed to stay clear of his wrath.

But as I turned away, he cuffed me—grabbed my sleeve—and leaned forward, his mouth close to my ear. "Things were diff'rent crewing for the Old Man. Nobody dared be late. And everybody worked harder than the next guy. We competed—culling, reefing, shoveling, whatever. It was a matter of pride—being the first aboard, first boat out, last boat in. And the Old Man worked me the hardest. Whenever he needed something, he shouted at me. 'Wade, reef that sail, 'Wade, lower the yawl boat. 'Wade, shovel them orsters back.' I believe he only knew one name on that boat—mine. He was either teaching me or trying to get me to quit. I think he wanted me to give up and go back to school." Murphy stopped talking for a moment to turn the wheel, then leaned toward me again, looked at the cabin, and lowered his voice. "See, I hated school and quit when I turned sixteen to crew on my father's skipjack, the *George W. Collier*. November 1957: first week of the season and the weather was bad. The wind was nor'east. Freezing rain. It rained the first day—ice-cold, drenching rain. Rained the second day. And the work was hard—two men lifting a four-hundred-pound drudge. By the third day it was still raining and I was ready to quit. School was looking good. But I stuck with it, the weather got better, and I grew to love sailing. Nothing like handling a skipjack. Crewed for the Old Man for seven years til I got my own boat. And here I am almost forty years later. Once you get it in your blood, it's hard to stop."

Dropping the air of co-conspiracy, he let go of my sleeve and returned to the helm.

About This Story

Naturalist and science writer Christopher White, once a staff biologist for the Chesapeake Bay Foundation, spent a year with three captains of wooden oystering sailboats to bring back the tales of oyster attrition and industry struggle he tells in his 2009 book, *Skipjack*. Oyster shells were once so abundant they were used as filler in roads and flux in iron furnaces, and they were pulverized into mortar, whitewash, and fertilizer. The town of Crisfield, Maryland, "the Crab Capital of the World," is literally built upon oyster shells. But diseases like MSX and dermo, in addition to overharvesting and pollution, have taken their toll. Oyster reefs formed from empty shells that accumulated over thousands of years were depleted in less than one hundred years. Today, though, oyster reefs are rebounding thanks to restoration projects across the Bay.

Take Harris Creek—a reef restoration project completed in 2015. This oyster reef, larger than the National Mall in Washington DC, was seeded with more than two billion oysters resistant to MSX and dermo, and the results have been promising. Reefs are typically monitored at three- and six-year marks, and in its first evaluation in 2018, Virginia Institute of Marine Science and the University of Maryland Center for Environmental Science found that the new 350-acre reef was able to filter the entire volume of water in Harris Creek in less than ten days. Their study concluded that the reef was providing a healthy habitat for other filter feeders like mussels and tunicates, which contribute 40 percent of the total filtration, and there was potential for removing one million pounds of nitrogen from the Bay over the next decade.

In 2021, nearly six billion shells were planted in ten select Chesapeake Bay tributaries, five in Maryland and five in Virginia. As of 2022, the Chesapeake Bay Program, leading the largest oyster restoration effort in the world, had restored 1,740 acres of oyster reef habitat in six of the ten tributaries. The group reported they were on track to meet their 2025 goal of restoring all ten tributaries.

Oyster shells are the best natural resource for rebuilding reefs but they are in short supply, so there are many efforts to involve residents in saving discarded shells to reuse in oyster restoration projects. Just one recycled oyster shell can offer habitat for ten baby oysters. Across Maryland, Virginia, and DC, programs like the Oyster

Recovery Partnership's Shell Recycling Alliance and the Chesapeake Bay Foundation's Save Oyster Shells collect shells from oyster roasts and seafood festivals, offer drop-off and pickup locations, and form partnerships with restaurants. The Chesapeake Bay Foundation's Oyster Gardening Program and the Oyster Recovery Partnership's Marylanders Grow Oysters program educate citizens who have dock access and provide them with supplies to grow oysters alongside their docks; the adult oysters are then planted on sanctuary reefs. Partnerships like this spanning businesses, nonprofits, and members of the community are breathing life back into the Chesapeake.

Reflections on a
York River Oyster

EMILY DECKER

I

Was it Swift who said
he was a bold man
that first ate an oyster?

I think it was a woman.
Who else could predict
the complexity
    of freshwater meeting salt,
the burden
    of filtering the Bay,
the palate and price
    of triggering desire,
and decide to swallow it all?

II

Protandric, adjective:
    having male reproductive organs
    while young

and female reproductive organs
later in a lifecycle

You know, then,
how to be everything
to yourself.

III
Shuck is such a word
You don't make it easy either,
do you—until you're pried
and opened?

IV
Our oystermen ancestors
lived by the tides,
like you and with you,
until you couldn't
and they couldn't,
and the Bay and its rivers
grew murkier
with your absence—
for a time.
But you've come
back to your beds now,
old and new.

About This Story
We couldn't conceive of a feminist oyster poem if we tried, but here
it is and we're so glad to have found it. We were moved by this poem

we came across in the 2023 *Bay to Ocean Journal: The Year's Best Writing from the Eastern Shore Writers Association* by Virginia native Emily Decker, a voice we had been searching for in a male-dominated industry and the literature that glorifies it. In a time when gender identity as it relates to biological sex is a divisive political issue, we find yet another example in nature of an organism that transitions from having male organs to female organs as a wholly natural cycle of life. We love the optimism in the poem's final observation, "you've come / back to your beds now," acknowledging the great efforts made toward rebuilding the oyster beds, overfished and emptied by disease. While many factors have contributed to the oysters' return—including harvest management and natural selection, as some oysters develop disease resistance—we want to highlight, in the spirit of this poem, the efforts of women in the industry.

Minorities in Aquaculture (MIA) is a nonprofit founded by Chestertown native Imani Black, whose family has been in the maritime industry for generations. "Working on the water is in my blood," Imani says. Often being the only woman in hatcheries, let alone a person of color, Imani recognized that the lack of diversity within her industry stemmed from the absence of people of color in *leadership* positions, not just the labor force. With this in mind, she wanted to build educational opportunities, community, and on-the-ground solutions to meaningfully engage people of color—especially Black women—in marine biology and aquaculture. MIA was launched in 2020 with the goal "to educate women of color on the environmental benefits of aquaculture and support them as they launch and sustain their careers in the field, growing the seafood industry and creating an empowering space for women along the way." Organizations like Imani's give us hope and a model for action.

The Geese

JAMES A. MICHENER

Excerpt from *Chesapeake*

In mid-September, as in each year of their lives, Onk-or and his mate felt irresistible urgings. They watched the sky and were particularly responsive to the shortening of the day. They noticed with satisfaction that their five children were large and powerful birds, with notable wing spans and sustaining accumulations of fat; they were ready for any flight. They also noticed the browning of the grasses and the ripening of certain seeds, signs unmistakable that departure was imminent.

At all the nests in the Arctic this restlessness developed and birds bickered with one another. Males would suddenly rise in the sky and fly long distances for no apparent reason, returning later to land in clouds of dust. No meetings were held; there was no visible assembling of families. But one day, for mysterious reasons which could not be explained, huge flocks of birds rose into the sky, milled about and then formed into companies heading south.

This southward migration was one of the marvels of nature: hundreds, thousands, millions of these huge geese forming into perfect V-shaped squadrons flying at different altitudes and at different times of day, but all heading out of Canada down one of the four principal flyways leading to varied corners of America. Some flew at 29,000 feet above the ground, others as low as 3,000, but all sought escape from the freezing moorlands of the Arctic, heading for clement feeding grounds like those in Maryland. For long spells they would fly in silence, but most often they maintained noisy communication, arguing, protesting, exulting, at night especially they uttered cries which echoed forever in the memories of men who heard them drifting down through the frosty air of autumn: *'Onk-or, onk-or!'*

The wedge in which Onk-or and his family started south this year consisted of eighty-nine birds, but it did not stay together permanently as a cohesive unit. Sometimes other groups would meld with it, until the flying formation contained several hundred birds; at other times segments would break away to fly with some other unit. But in general the wedge held together.

The geese flew at a speed of about forty-five miles an hour, which meant that if they stayed aloft for an entire day, they could cover a thousand miles. But they required rest, and through the centuries during which they had followed the same route south and north they had learned of various ponds and lakes and riverbanks which afforded them secure places to rest and forage. There were lakes in upper Quebec, and small streams leading into the St. Lawrence. In Maine there were hundreds of options and suitable spots in western Massachusetts and throughout New York, and the older geese like Onk-or knew them all.

On some days, near noon when the autumn sun was high, the geese would descend abruptly and alight on a lake which their ancestors had been utilizing for thousands of years. The trees along the shore would have changed, and new generations of fish would occupy the waters, but the seeds would be the same kind, and the succulent grasses. Here the birds would rest for six or seven hours, and then as dusk approached, the leaders would utter signals and the flock would scud across the surface of the lake, wheel into the air and fly aloft. There they would form themselves automatically into a long V, with some old, sage bird like Onk-or in the lead, and through the night they would fly south.

Maine, New Hampshire, Massachusetts, Connecticut, New York, Pennsylvania! The states would lie sleeping below, only a few dim lamps betraying their existence, and overhead the geese would go, crying in the night *'Onk-or, onk-or,'* and occasionally, at the edge of some village or on some farm a door would open and light would flood the area for a while, and parents would hold their children and peer into the dark sky, listening to the immortal passing of the geese. And once in a great while, on such a night, when the moon was full, the children would actually see the flying wedge pass between them and the moon, and hear the geese as they flew, and this matter they would speak of for the rest of their lives.

No goose, not even a powerful one like Onk-or, could fly at the head of the wedge for long periods. The buffeting of the wind as the point of the V broke a path through the air turbulence was too punishing. The best a practiced bird could do was about forty minutes, during which time he absorbed a considerable thrashing. After his allotted time in the lead position, the exhausted goose would drop to the back of one of the arms of the wedge, where the weaker birds had been assembled, and there, with the air well broken ahead of him, he would coast along in the wake of the others, recovering his strength until it came his time again to assume the lead. Male and female alike accepted this responsibility, and when the day's flight ended, they were content to rest. On especially favorable lakes with copious feed they might stay for a week.

During the first days of October the geese were usually somewhere in New York or Pennsylvania, and happy to be there. The sun was warm and the lakes congenial, but as the northwest winds began to blow, bringing frost at night, the older birds grew restive. They did not relish a sudden freeze, which would present problems, and they vaguely knew that the waning of the sun required them to be farther south in some region of security.

But they waited until the day came when the air was firmly frosted, and then they rose to form their final V. No matter where the lake had been upon which they were resting, the geese in the eastern flyway vectored in to the Susquehanna River, and when they saw its broad and twisting silhouette, they felt safe. This was their immemorial guide, and they followed it with assurance, breaking at last onto the Chesapeake, the most considerable body of water they would see during their migration. It shimmered in the autumn sun and spoke of home. Its thousand estuaries and coves promised them food and refuge for the long winter, and they loved to see it.

As soon as the Chesapeake was reached, congregations of geese began to break off, satisfied that they had arrived at their appointed locations. Four thousand would land at Havre de Grace, twenty thousand at the Sassafras. The Chester River would lure more than a hundred thousand and the Miles the same. Enormous concentrations would elect Tred Avon, but the most conspicuous aggregation would wait for the Choptank, more than a quarter of a million birds, and they would fill every field and estuary.

For more than five thousand years Onk-or's lineal antecedents had favored a marsh on the north bank of the Choptank. It was spacious, well-grassed with many plants producing seeds, and multiple channels providing safe hiding places. It was convenient both to fields, so that the geese could forage for seeds, and to the river, so that they could land and take off easily. It was an ideal wintering home in every respect but one: it was owned by the

Turlocks, the most inveterate hunters of Maryland, each member of the family born with an insatiable appetite for goose.

'I can eat it roasted, or chopped with onions and peppers, or sliced thin with mushrooms,' Lafe Turlock was telling the men at the store. 'You can keep the other months of the year, just give me November with a fat goose comin' onto the stove three times a week.'

Lafe had acquired from his father and his father before him the secrets of hunting geese. 'Canniest birds in the world. They have a sixth sense, a seventh and an eighth. I've seen one smart old gander haunts my place lead his flock right into my blind, spot my gun, stop dead in the air, turn his whole congregation around on a six-pence, without me gettin' a shot.' He kicked the stove and volunteered his summary of the situation: 'A roast goose tastes so good because it's so danged hard to shoot.'

'Why's that?' a younger hunter asked.

Lafe turned to look at the questioner, studied him contemptuously as an interloper, then explained, 'I'll tell you what, sonny, I know your farm down the river. Fine farm for huntin' geese. Maybe a hundred thousand fly past in the course of a week, maybe two hundred thousand. But that ain't doin' you no good, because unless you can tease just one of those geese to drop down within gunshot of where you stand, you ain't never gonna kill a goose. They fly over there'—he flailed his long arms—'or over here, or down there, a hundred thousand geese in sight...' He startled the young man by leaping from his chair and banging his fist against the wall. 'But never one goddamned goose where you want him. It's frustratin'.'

He sat down, cleared his throat and spoke like a lawyer presenting a difficult case. 'So what you got to do, sonny, is pick yourself a likely spot where they might land, and build yourself a blind—'

'I done that.'

Lafe ignored the interruption. 'And hide it in branches that look live, and all round it put wooden decoys whittled into at least eight different positions to look real, and then learn to yell goose cries that would fool the smartest goose ever lived. And if you don't do all these things, sonny, you ain't never gonna taste goose, because they gonna fly past you, night and day.'

The attractive thing about Lafe was his unquenchable enthusiasm. Each October, like now, he was convinced that this year he would outsmart the geese, and he was not afraid to make his predictions public at the store. 'This year, gentlemen, you all eat goose. I'm gonna shoot so many, your fingers'll grow warts pluckin' 'em.'

'That's what you said last year,' an uncharitable waterman grunted.

'But this year I got me a plan. And with a finger dipped in molasses he started to outline his strategy. You know my blind out in the river.'

'I stood there often enough, gettin' nothin',' one of the men said.

'And you know this blind at that pond in the western end of the marsh.'

'I waited there for days and all I got was a wet ass,' the same man said.

'And that's what you'll get in that blind this year, too. Because I'm settin' them two up just like always, decoys and all. I want that smart old leader to see them and lead his ladies away.'

'To where?' the skeptic asked.

Lafe grinned and a deep satisfaction wreathed his face. 'Now for my plan. Over here, at the edge of this cornfield where everythin looks so innicent, I plant me a third blind with the best decoys me or my pappy ever carved.' And with a dripping finger he allowed the molasses to form his new blind.

'I don't think it'll work,' the cynic said.

'I'm gonna get me so many geese...'

'Like last year. How many you get last year, speak honest.'

'I got me nine geese ...' In six months he had shot nine geese, but this year, with his new tactics, he was sure to get scores.

So when Onk-or brought his wedge of eighty-nine back to the Choptank marshes, dangerous innovations awaited. Of course, on his first pass over Turlock land he spotted the traditional blind in the river and the ill-concealed one at the pond; generations of his family had been avoiding those inept seductions. He also saw the same old decoys piled on the bank, the boats waiting to take the hunters into the river and the dogs waiting near the boats. It was familiar and it was home.

Giving a signal, he dropped in a tight, crisp circle, keeping his left wing almost stationary, then landed with a fine splashing on an opening in the center of the marsh. He showed his five children how to dispose themselves, then pushed his way through the marsh grass to see for himself what feed there might be in the fields. His mate came along, and within a few minutes they had satisfied themselves that this was going to be a good winter. On their way back to the marsh they studied the cabin. No changes there; same wash behind the kitchen.

As the geese settled in to enjoy the marshes, the young birds heard for the first time the reverberation of gunfire, and Onk-or had to spend much time alerting them to the special dangers that accompanied these rich feeding grounds. He and the other ganders taught the newcomers how to spot the flash of metal, or hear the cracking of a twig under a gunner's boot. And no group must ever feed without posting at least three sentinels, whose job it was to keep their necks erect so that their ears and eyes could scout all approaches.

Eternal vigilance was the key to survival, and no birds ever became more skilled in protecting themselves. Smaller birds, like doves, which presented difficult targets for a hunter, could often trust to luck that an undetected human would miss when he fired at them, but the great goose presented such an attractive target either head-on or broadside that a gunner had the advantage, if he were allowed to creep within range. The trick for the geese was to move out of range whenever men approached, and Onk-or drilled his flock assiduously in this tactic, for any goose who frequented the Turlock marshes was threatened by some of the most determined hunters on the Eastern Shore.

By mid-December it was clear that the geese had outsmarted Lafe Turlock once again; none had landed at the blind in the river and only a few stragglers had landed at the pond. By the end of the first week Onk-or had spotted the cornfield trick, and Lafe had been able to shoot only three geese.

'Them damn honkers must of got eyeglasses in Canada,' he told the men at the store.

About This Story

Judging by its size alone, one might expect James A. Michener's 1978 novel *Chesapeake* to be the textbook on the Chesapeake Bay. Described as a classic and a "most ambitious work of fiction in theme and scope," Michener's book follows a character who, fleeing from religious persecution, sets sail on Captain John Smith's voyage across seas and is present at the creation of a new nation. Its eight hundred pages span four hundred years in the region, largely around the Bay and the Choptank River, from the first landing on America's shores all the way to the 1970s. The reader encounters Native Americans, pirates, Quakers, slaves, abolitionists, and politicians along the way.

Michener's *The Watermen*, which we discovered at a local library's used book sale, is made up of excerpts from the larger novel.

Despite watermen being a central theme to the Bay, we were drawn to share this story of a flock of geese and the migration ritual that has occurred for thousands of years. Every January since the 1960s, the US Fish and Wildlife Service has teamed up with the Maryland Department of Natural Resources for a midwinter survey that counts the population of waterfowl along the shorelines of the Chesapeake in Maryland, the tidal Potomac River, and the Atlantic coast. The western and eastern shores of the Chesapeake Bay are favorite wintering spots for resident and migratory Canada geese, who descend in the fall and then in late winter or early spring move north again along the Atlantic Flyway to their breeding grounds in the northern United States and Canada, making both populations prime targets for hunters. But the population of geese has been increasing steadily as they have grown accustomed to the Bay, learning to eat bay grasses in the shallows and even breeding in the area. Marking the changing of seasons, the Piscataway-Conoy Tribe has long celebrated the arrival of migrating Canada geese to Maryland with the Greeting of the Geese event at the Merkle Wildlife Sanctuary. The event includes a day of dancing, crafts, and demonstrations led by the tribe—and even a presentation of ancient oyster roasting techniques. If you're in the area, we hope you will join them to say hello to our friend Onk-or.

The Henning Tides

CURTIS J. BADGER

*Excerpt from Salt Tide: Currents of Nature
and Life on the Virginia Coast*

My father and I were alone in a small cedar skiff, waiting for the marsh to flood. We could see the ocean break over the dunes of the barrier islands, and we could hear the violence of the open water as the offshore sandbar slowed its pace, forcing it to tumble onto the berm of the beach, white plumes of salt spray skittering across the sand.

But where we were, in a leeward marsh protected by the islands, the water was calm and silent, running in strong, deep currents through the narrow creeks that laced the salt marsh.

The water rose almost imperceptibly, first covering the bases of the marsh plants, climbing slowly to the salt rim that marked the normal level of high tide, and then continuing to rise, covering the shorter grasses and obscuring the winding creeks and guts, until finally there was no marsh, but a flat expanse of building water where only patches of high grass showed. The ocean inlet between the islands, the shallow bay that separated the islands and the mainland, and the marshes were all as one, covered with water from the barrier island dunes to the line of trees on the distant mainland.

The moon was full, and the pull of the moon's gravity tugged the water toward the land. A northeast storm was offshore, and its winds pushed the ocean as the moon's gravity pulled, sending the breakers far up the beach, over the islands in low areas, and into the marshes and the forests and fields of the mainland.

I sat on a rough board bench in the bow of the skiff, holding my father's old shotgun across my lap, and I watched the tide rise, felt its silent power against the hull of the boat, which my father held steady in the current with a long oak push pole. I wondered about the tide. What if it were not to crest? What if it were to continue beyond the time of high water, and what if instead of soon ebbing, it continued to rise, even if only for a few hours? Already the marsh had been covered, the landscape erased, familiar benchmarks removed, all reference to solid land gone. The woods and fields would be next, and the houses and farms, the small towns and businesses, schools, churches. And I realized how our lives are governed by cycles such as the rising and falling of the tide, how we trust in the precision and predictability of natural events. Afloat on a flooding tide, I realize how precarious life is, how subject to sudden change, how fragile and fleeting, how dependent upon a process that has no margin for error.

It was September, and the northeast wind carried the first cold insinuations of winter. My father and I were alone. On the open water there were no other boats, none for miles. I sat in the bow of the skiff and nervously fingered the double-barreled shotgun, clicking the safety switch on and off, on and off. I felt in my pocket for the shells; I shuffled them with my hand and it made me feel warmer, shells tightly packed and heavy with powder and lead, their brass bases clicking together in a satisfying way.

It was time, my father said. He stood and planted the long push pole into the flooded marsh, and the boat pressed forward. He told me to load the gun, and I slid in two shells and snapped it shut, checking the safety switch. My father poled the boat along the edge of a flooded salt marsh gut. Grass grows higher on the edge of a gut because it is fed by the twice-daily flush of the tides. In the flooded marsh, wisps of green grass remained above water, defining the meandering path of the guts. My father pushed the boat through these green grasstops, and I sat in the bow with the gun, watching the grass fifty yards ahead of us, looking for the bobbing heads of clapper rails, which we called marsh hens.

My father saw the first one, which was not swimming ahead of us but off to the side, attempting to flank us and get behind us. It was in the open water, bobbing and weaving, no grass in which to hide. As I lifted the gun, the rail reluctantly flushed, its wings stirring the surface of the still water. My shot peppered the water around the bird, creating an ellipse of foam. The shot seemed unnaturally loud and out of place in this marsh where the only sound was the rumble of distant waves. The marsh hen lay on its back, kicking its leg. I raised the gun to shoot again, but my father leaned forward and pressed his hand on my shoulder and I took the gun down. He pushed the boat to the bird and I picked it up, dead now, eyes glazing, wet but warm, much larger than I had expected, soft, all neck and legs, subtle browns and grays, tiny head and long bill.

My first bird. I must have been thirteen. It's a good tide, my father said, by way of congratulations.

The current had stopped flowing, and the tide crested at seven feet above mean low water. A good marsh henning tide. We had consulted the tide table the day before, knowing that the full moon would produce a tide of about six feet above mean low. But the northeaster offshore turned a marginal henning tide into an extraordinary one.

You get these tides only a few times a year, when moon phase and weather conspire to drive the tide higher than normal, covering all but the tallest grasses of the highest marsh. The marsh hens, which normally have thousands of acres of tall grass in which to hide, become vulnerable for perhaps two hours, just before the crest of the tide and just after. So my father poled the boat along the grassy rim and I shot marsh hens, and then I poled the boat and my father shot, and as the morning grew old the sun warmed us and the tide began to fall. And as the tide fell we left the skiff and walked the high marsh, flushing rail birds from tumps of grass. By noon we filled our limits of fifteen birds each and started home.

I was wet from the waist down from walking the marsh, and as we crossed the bay and made our way back to the mainland, the wind stung. The rail birds were in a basket in the bottom of the boat, and a trickle of seawater ran from them and from my wet feet, forming a pool there. A chop was running in the bay, and as the skiff plowed into the waves, the breeze would carry the spray over me, soaking me to the skin.

My first hunting trip, a seaside baptism of full immersion, I thought, an introduction to the discomforting reality that in order for me to live, something else must die. That night our family had marsh hens for dinner. They had a wonderful wild taste, milder than wild duck, but with the flavor of the marsh: slightly salty, slightly fishlike.

I was proud of having killed these birds, of having helped feed our family. It was the directness of the process of life and death, the unbending reality of it, that made its impression upon me. My father and I went out in a flooding tide and killed food for the family, much as a hawk might, or a fox, or, for that matter, a marsh hen as it plucks a grasshopper from a blade of Spartina grass. I felt, in a vague and uncertain way, that I knew nature better by having participated in it, eliminating the cattle ranches, poultry farms, slaughterhouses, and grocery markets that turn the daily business of living and dying into an unseen and abstract concept. Would I have felt the same pride had I spent the day mowing my neighbors' lawns and then taken the money to the corner grocery and exchanged it for chicken or steak? Is it more moral or less moral to kill your own dinner, or to pay someone to do it for you?

In the salt marsh on that September morning, morality was not an issue, yet I knew that the violent act of ending a bird's life was heavy with implications. It was different from catching fish or clams, even though those acts also meant the death of a flounder or shellfish. Perhaps it was the violence and finality of the shot, the decision to pull the trigger, the letting of blood. It signified something, as in Isaac MacCaslin's first worthy blood in Faulkner's *The Bear*: the symbolic abandonment of childhood, a rite of passage charged with certain indelible emotions that remain with you throughout life. After many marsh henning tides, death has not become common, not without silent reverence, thankfulness, and pride—emotions I never have felt at the supermarket checkout counter.

I have come to love rail birds because they remind me that I am not above nature, but a part of it. If I destroy their marsh, they will be gone, and in the rails' absence, marsh henning tides will have no relevance, no currency, and the value of my life will be just as diminished as theirs. So the point is to protect those places that sustain rail birds, in order that a few might sustain me.

My father was my age when he first took me rail hunting. When my son is thirteen or so, I will take him rail hunting. I'll be the age my father was when he took me. Old, I thought at the time. I worried about my father as he poled the skiff. He worked in an office. What if he had a heart attack?

But my father lived to be eighty-two and died only recently. I was with him as he lay dying, and I thought not of my grief and my loss, but of marsh henning tides, of moon gravity, and of the precious, dependable cycle of ebb and flood.

My father died at 2:10 P.M. on a hot July day in a hospital emergency room. The time seems important to me. In the emergency room there was a large, white clock that, amid the clutter of very expensive medical equipment, seemed to dominate everything else. No one in the room was keeping track of the time, but time was to me the real focus.

Time is measured in precious seconds for a man with a bullet in his chest or for one severely injured in an auto accident. With each second, an injured man grows nearer to death, and it is the doctors' challenge to beat the clock, to stabilize the trauma, to reverse the inertia of dying.

For my father, there was nothing to stabilize, no life and death fight for the clock to referee. The walls of the aorta near his heart had given way, had ruptured like a worn tire, too weak to patch, too worn to function. His kidneys were failing. He lay on a narrow table, surrounded by machines that temporarily substituted for his falling body. He wore pale blue hospital pajamas, open across his white chest, which was stained with blood and antiseptics where the tubes had been inserted. The machines and the tubes held his life in suspension, not in order that the doctors could perform repairs, but so I could get there to say goodbye.

I had been on the boat, and it had been raining, so we came in early and found the message from the doctor. He used the word "grave" to describe my father's condition, but I knew even without that word that my father was approaching a moment for which he had been preparing for weeks. He had not planned his death, but he felt it coming and had given himself up to it, sometimes bitterly, but without drama and pretense.

We had not spoken of his impending death, as though if we did not acknowledge its nearness, it would go away. So, even as the clock ticked away the seconds in the emergency room, we did not speak of death. He smiled when he saw me, and I told him he was going to be all right. There were no final messages. We both were aware of what was imminent. My father had weeks ago left his room at the retirement home where he lived and moved into the hospital wing, tired, unwilling to eat, growing astonishingly weaker and older and more resigned each day. We both knew without speaking of it what he was doing. His final gesture of reluctance came in the emergency room. "Can I go back to my room now?" he asked.

His death came without pain. Freed from the pumps and electrical circuits that prolonged both life and death, he slowly retreated. I stroked his head and wept and watched the shallowing arcs on the heart monitor.

My father was eighty-two. He had lived a rich life, chasing no wild ambitions, enjoying the simple pleasures of fishing and hunting and growing vegetables in his garden. He spent his life doing work he felt important. He served his community, loved and supported his family, and believed in God, although he did nothing at the end to invoke the supernatural. Perhaps, as in other aspects of his life, he had done that earlier, in private.

When my father had weeks earlier begun his ritual of dying, I had resented his lack of fight, his resignation. He would not eat, would not care for himself. He had always been a dapper dresser, but now he went around in soiled shirts. His socks did not match.

I talked with our family doctor and arranged various examinations, hoping for a cure to something that had no remedy. He was eighty-two. He was tired. So in the end, I too became resigned, or more accurately, accepting.

Sharing my father's death with him assuaged my grief and brought release to both of us. It brought enlightenment as well, eliminating some of the mystery and fear, the bitterness, confusion, and frustration. The despair I had earlier felt gradually gave way as I realized that what my father felt was not resignation, but metamorphosis, an inevitable modulation of body and spirit, a union of the abstract with the real.

I imagine that my father's death was much like that of his father. I have a dim image of my grandfather in his final days, his thin, white hair combed back, his white mustache neatly trimmed, his high cheekbones made more prominent by illness. He died at his home, with my father at his side, and I doubt that they spoke of death and life, or of love and grief. I'm sure my grandfather taught my father about death, just as my father taught me some forty years later. Like my father and me, they would coyly have failed to acknowledge death's presence, until it came and set them free.

I held my father's head and I watched the wall clock, and at the moment of his death the clock read ten past two. It's odd that I should remember the wall clock, so huge that it seemed surreal. But it was fitting, I think, that as I said goodbye to my father I was thinking of rail birds, of the salt marsh, and of our first hunt together.

In the flooded marsh those many years ago, with the moon's gravity coaxing the ocean onto the mainland, was my father teaching me to be a hunter? Or was he preparing me for this last day, and for one that will in time come to me? Was he, too, thinking of rail birds and marsh henning tides?

About This Story

While Badger's story takes place on the Atlantic side of Virginia's Eastern Shore, where his family has lived since the 1600s, the landscape and culture neighbors and mirrors the Chesapeake's fascination with waterfowl hunting. In our research, we regularly noted the hunting motifs and museums all around the Chesapeake, but we struggled to connect to this locally beloved pastime. Not only did hunting prohibit us from visiting many parks that were just beginning their hunting season, it puzzled us as non-hunters. How could someone who loves these birds also *shoot* them? Sure, we acknowledge that humans have hunted for sustenance for centuries . . . but for sport? It was Badger's writing that prompted us to think differently.

Featuring this excerpt after Michener's "The Geese" allows us to show two sides of the story—the great bird migration from Onk-or's point of view, and the ritual of shooting marsh hens from a hunter's point of view. Both, we realized, are part of the heritage and traditions of a place like the Chesapeake Bay. Badger's story wonders about the precarity of life and the morality of death. By starting with the death of the marsh hen and ending with the death of his father, he shows us that we are not apart from nature; we are in fact a part of it. This piece helped us see the connection hunters have to the land and water, their keen awareness of tides and times, the bonds hunting can form among people—and how all of these connections forge a strong appreciation for and desire to protect special places. In many instances, conservation efforts are rooted in hunting. The driving force behind many habitat and wildlife protection efforts is a commitment to ensure the future population of wildlife to hunt.

The National Wildlife Refuge System was founded by President Theodore Roosevelt in 1903 with the purpose of conserving native species dependent on a diverse network of lands and water, and supporting compatible wildlife-dependent recreation like fishing, hunting, hiking, and wildlife viewing. The Migratory Bird Conservation Act of 1929 authorized the federal government to acquire and preserve wetlands as waterfowl habitat, and the Duck Stamp Act passed in 1934 provided a source of funds to buy these properties through the sale of the Federal Duck Stamp. Sales have protected millions of acres of habitat, allowing the National Wildlife Refuge System to acquire key breeding, migration, and wintering habitat for migratory birds, and benefiting other wildlife species and habitats. As of 2024, the network included 570 refuges spanning 95 million acres of land and 760 million acres of marine habitat across fifty states and five US territories—welcoming more than 67 million visitors each year, only 2.63 million of them there to hunt.

Susquehanna Down

TOM WISNER AND MARK WISNER

Original story and song from *Follow on the Water*

It's interesting to think of life like an ongoing series of resurrections. To think I came to Solomon's Island to lay down my sword and shield. Come home to water, home from the fire, home to work at Chesapeake Biology Lab. Home from Korea, home from college and biology jobs and other places and times. Home to work at peace, making peace with the river. Home to awaken the life of the river, into the eyes of my people. Well actually, first in my own eyes and then perhaps in the eyes of my people.

I'm thinkin' right this moment that it was all about resurrections. Resurrection of the life of the Patuxent River. I would become rivers goin' to the sea. I would follow on these waters in my own way. I heard my waterman son Mark singing his lines *"Susquehanna down to ocean waters in Virginia. You'll carry on into the eyes of my child"* And I knew then that he was resurrecting life. Singin' life up from the dark, dark time of our rivers.

> *Cold and clear, are the Chesapeake Waters*
> *Free are the men who dare to respect her*
> *Susquehanna down to ocean waters in Virginia*
> *You'll carry on to the eyes of my child . . . .*

There was an old woman, her name was Captain Susanna Brins-field—used to live down at Solomons Island. And her time here in the early part of the last century, she was the skipper, the schooner ward. A genuine Chesapeake women's libber.

She was born a Langley—the aunt of Reds and Pepper Lang-ley—raised up over in St Mary's County on Flat Iron Road. She married 'ol Captain Brinsfield in the Seven Gables Hotel, that's just across from Solomons, when she was right young. After that wedding, they came over to the island aboard the bugeye. It was his bugeye, actually. Brinsfield was also the owner and skipper of the schooner ward so in that marriage, she became its co-owner and they sailed cargo all over the bay. Pumpkins and peaches up to Baltimore from southern Maryland in the fall. Coal oil and lantern fuels back to the South in the winter. Great loads of farm produce and lumber at all other times of year.

The legend has it that after 'ol man Brinsfield died, she became the skipper of the ward. The white crew deserted her as they refused to sail with a woman. And she hired on all Black crew and continued to work the Chesapeake for her remaining active years.

Susie was well into her nineties when I knew her. Slight of frame, no bigger than a chicken. She lived in a small one room cabin near where the modern day bridge sits now. The old schooner ward was rotting away in the upper reaches of Back Creek behind her cabin. Many folks would say, "That 'ol boat was driv' up shoal up in some 'ol gut to die." That's the way most of these 'ol boats would go back into the elements. A boat is sort of like us in that way. But 'ol Susie, she wasn't driv' up shoal. She was still very much involved in bein' alive.

Her face had actually become covered in this bumpy sclero-derma from many years in the sun. She had these small piercing beady eyes that would bore a hole right through you. I used to love to listen to her stories of old times out on the river. Sometimes when she'd speak to me, I felt as though I was being enchanted by this ancient vestige of a wise old turtle made over into an old woman, and come here from the sea. She could tell all the 'ol tales of northern schooners *"come down here to steal oysters above Lore's bar!"* She told me stories of fisher folks and leaving home, weaving nets, patchin' up the sails, and catchin' things from the bottom to sell dock-side. She was a livin' history of the island way of life.

I used to have fun with Susie askin' her foolish questions like *"Susie what did folks do in the old days when you got depressed, unhappy, messed up and there were no psychoanalysts or groups around to help you get back on board?"* She looked puzzled at me and she'd say *"What you do is just be happy! Just be happy. There ain't no sense in bein' sad. Yessir!"* she'd say. *"Yessir!"* I loved that little *"Yessir!"* she put on the ends of just about everything she'd say. I used to love to kid her, askin' *"How'd you live to be so old?"* She'd say *"It's 'da Lord that's keepin' me here, and I sure do hope it's for a good purpose. Yessir! I sure do hope it's for a good purpose". . . .*

One cold December day, I was drivin' down to the island on the main road. And it actually started to snow. There were flakes coming down as big as silver dollars. They were floatin' down all around and I saw Susie outside her cabin choppin' wood with an axe as big as she was, so I pulled over. I got out of the car and picked up a spare axe by the pile and man, I started helpin' her. I was in my best form, in my 40's and I was fit. I loved bustin' up those blocks. Susie was doin' real good at that too. And my Uncle Roy used to say, *"There's a whole lot of fun in that wood pile, Tommy!"* Susie and I, we kept at it and in fair time we laid up a good stick of wood. It was getting windy and the snow... the snow was really pilin' up. A real damp chill was settling in on us so I said *"Susie, let's go in that cabin and get a cup of coffee and sit and talk a while."* She looked at me, incredulous with those penetrating little eyes all squinty and bored right into me... and she said *"There ain't no way you comin' into that cabin with me... alone!"*

> *Susie, Susanne sailed the Bay like her 'ol man*
> *from Baltimore, bringin' down a load of coal*
> *Bustin' down the bay, with all the sail she can handle,*
> *Smile on her face, be in Solomons by morn'.*
>
> *Cold and clear, are the Chesapeake Waters*
> *Free are the men who dare to respect her*
> *Susquehanna down to ocean waters in Virginia*
> *You'll carry on to the eyes of my child*

My son Mark worked aboard the *Howard* for Captain Stan Daniels out of Deals Island, Maryland. Captain Stan was a tough skipper, bound to get his take of oysters on any day of work. Mark said, "When you'd work with Stan, you'd be driv' hard and put up wet." That was a hard go, aboard the *Howard*. That crew had their own version of the Lord's prayer, they'd say "Our Father, who art in heaven, *Howard* be thy name."

> *There's Cap'in Stan, strength of youth still within him,*
> *when his voice roars, that old cooky shuts his door.*
> *Come ice or snow, or the north wind before him,*
> *come the break of day, a dredgin' he will go*

That last line in the verse where Captain Stan says *"a dredgin' he will go,"* Captain Watt used to say, *"You people call it a dredge but if you'da worked it like I did, you'd call it a drudge for sure!"* Most of the Bay folk, they do call it that. . . .

These wood boats of sails have been in the Chesapeake since the island folks arrived here from England and started cuttin' the forest and built their homes, sheds and their boats. The large chain and metal dredges brought into the bay by Connecticut Yankees around year 1810, they were fixed to large hand-wound winches of ships on bateaus, and schooners and bugeyes. A whole culture arose and grew life into our Chesapeake island homes. These old boats are, they're you know... living things, they're made of wood and the fibers of hemp made to rope and cotton wove to canvas to put before their mast and take on life and fly before the wind. And they were skippered by men who'd spend their lives aboard of them, flying out before the wind. Wooden boat and man became an expression of the same life of Chesapeake. The Bay and its bounty provided a generous lifelong feast, and those who worked that bounty were generous to a fault.

Captain Art Daniels is a genuine expression of the people of Middle Bay country. He's a great sailor and a dredger, a fine tenor singer, a generous friend and above all... surely, he's a man of the Lord.

> *There's Captain Art, he's a Deal Island dredger*
> *No man alive knows this bay any better*
> *Preaches the Lord, and loves a good sailin' weather*
> *Speaks from his heart and smiles from his eyes.*

Cold and clear, are the Chesapeake Waters
Free are the men who dare to respect her
Susquehanna down to ocean waters in Virginia
You'll carry on to the eyes of my child.

About This Story

Tom Wisner—folk singer, educator, environmentalist, and activist—was known as the Bard of the Chesapeake. We stumbled upon his name in various publications citing his poetry and folk songs, which advocate for celebrating, preserving, and educating people about the Chesapeake waters and way of life. Though there were many songs we wanted to include, we chose this track entitled "Susquehanna Down" from his album *Follow on the Water*, telling Susanna Brinsfield's story interspersed with a song by Tom's son, Mark Wisner, because it honors his dedication to giving voice to the unrecognized and voiceless—the Chesapeake waters, its living creatures, and in this case, the *women* who were a part of its history and legacy, too.

Tom Wisner didn't just write poems and songs about the people of the Chesapeake—he painted and photographed them, and recorded their stories, too. "If you want to know the Chesapeake, Tom Wisner's final album, *Follow on the Water*, will make you mourn all you've missed," read the *Bay Weekly* review, and that album became the soundtrack of our visit. His music weaves together connections he made over a lifetime in this region, first growing up outside of DC and then working in a biology lab on Solomon's Island. Wisner said, "We're bound in a web of deep and mysterious relations with the souls of other creatures. With periwinkles, crabs, fish, goose, turtle and others. We live at all times in the shade of their presence here. They are the wonderful elements of the creation that haunt, nourish and guide our lives: the terrapin, the great blue heron and relentless old watermen."

Wisner's songs have become teaching tools and anthems, too. His son shared with us, "His life's work centered around education. Tom believed if he could bring a student to love a topic of study, they would own the process, and take it to new levels. He dedicated his life to the preservation of the waters and the land of Chesapeake Bay." His first album, *Chesapeake Born*, was recorded with Mark on the Smithsonian Folkways label and includes the beloved song of the same name. His posthumous collection *Singing the Chesapeake* compiles songs he sang often with children and groups of educators throughout the region. A friend shared with the *Bay Weekly* that he even videotaped movements that go with his song "Freedom Is a River" to "encourage singing and motion with disabled folks."

Mark shared that his father "had a great respect not only for the creatures in the Bay, but also for the heritage and culture surrounding it." Tom's song "Bernie's Measure" celebrates the Patuxent River Wade-In, a beloved tradition started by Maryland state senator Bernie Fowler to promote improving water quality in the Bay. Each year, Marylanders wade into the water and see how far they can go before losing sight of their sneakers, a measure that has come to be known as the sneaker index. As the executive director of the Chesapeake Bay Commission shared with the *Bay Journal*, "The wade-in was just a beautiful example where Bernie combined science with community involvement. He made his sneakers a scientific tool, a Secchi disk. And then he combined it with politicians and music and floats and picnics. Because he knew if you're going to accomplish environmental protection it has to be fun."

Elegy for a Chesapeake Fish House

AUDREY Y. SCHARMEN

Excerpt from *Arpeggio of Redwings*

So venerable, so vulnerable

The building clings stubbornly to its place beside the wide mouth of a river that feeds into the Chesapeake. It is a typical crab house, purveyor of Bay bounty, a very old sprawling farm structure once encircled by wetlands of willow and mallows and rushes. Now the wetlands are occupied by new upscale buildings with trendy Palladian windows like arched eyebrows that lend a perpetual expression of disdain to the facades. They stare haughtily at the shabby old-timer, as if questioning his right to be there.

The old place has a wonderful wraparound porch with wooden tables where we sit in summer to watch the river run. It is a friendly refuge where mallards, rowdy as small children, race about the table legs and mingle with diners. These ducks are descendants of those we first met many years ago on this porch, hatched amid the pink petunias and marigolds in whiskey barrels beside the front door.

At sunset, we watch the gaudy remnants of the day promenade across the horizon, littering the water with glittering scraps and casting a rosy glow on a lone egret bound homeward. The mallards, suddenly grown sedate at twilight, murmur drowsily as they make the final rounds of tables and greet patrons or pause to annoy the gull with the broken wing who is mending here on the porch.

Schools of stripers come to beg at the railing where the waves bound off the pilings. They are big beautiful fish, frolicking on the surface as they snap up breadcrumbs. We lean precariously over the rail to marvel at their behavior: nobility begging like feral cats at the fish house door.

So it is that we linger longer than usual on our last night beside the river, in the glow of starlight with a hint of autumn in the air, to ponder the fate of fish houses and porches, of crabs and oysters and beggar stripers. So much a part of the Chesapeake is this venerable building: a kind of earthbound reef long nurtured by spot and roe and megalops. A refuge of mallards and mending gulls, a place of torn screens and picnic tables spread with faded oilcloth, a homely place redolent of crab and creosote and cigarettes. A way of life.

When we return next summer to this broad, wandering stream with the sweet breath of the sea, there may be only the crowd of Palladian faces to greet us—triumphantly blocking our way to the tomb of an old friend, one we took too much for granted.

—August 30, 1995

Autumn Sharpens Our Senses

AUDREY Y. SCHARMEN

Excerpt from *Arpeggio of Redwings*

We grow alert to what is here and what is going

Around the autumnal equinox, the season reveals itself in subtle ways. No matter the place, autumn's advent is defined by a certain aura that brings a quickening of the senses—anticipation tinged with melancholy. And so it is here in Chesapeake Country.

The goldenrod blooms and the first crimson leaf from my ash tree appears magically on the front doormat—like a calling card—filling me with unease. I need to grasp summer's shirttail as it slips away. I need to see the golden meadows of late summer cosmos, the crimson-eyed rose mallows thick in the salt marshes, the wild clematis that wanders restlessly along wooded bands. I need to follow the haunting summer song of the Chesapeake that beckons me seaward.

We unslip the *Cardinal* for our cruising adventure.

Crossing the Bay to launch from Crisfield on the rising tide, we thread our way through the winding marshes of Broad Creek and across capricious Pocomoke Sound toward a 10,000-acre wetland Eden, Shad Landing, in Pocomoke River State Park.

A thin river winds a dark and deep course from the Sound to Snow Hill through 30 scenic miles of salt marshes until dwindling to a trickle a few miles from the waters of Chincoteague.

This is the Pocomoke River, a mystical place where great hardwoods and feathery cypress conjure fantasies of wood nymphs and fairies. Eagles, herons, kingfishers, flycatchers and warblers thrive in this opulent wilderness. Such spots aren't to be hurried; this is a slow day's cruise.

Our old Chris-Craft cruiser takes us all the way to the upper river. She is well behaved, maintaining a leisurely pace and controlling her wake to keep from disturbing the delicate shoreline and tributary tranquility. The *Cardinal* clears bridges that bar tall-masted sailors. If the captain keeps a sharp eye out, she'll also avoid the sand barges that travel back and forth between Shelltown and Pocomoke City.

Fair-weather cumulonimbus clouds in a bright blue sky accompany us all the way. At Shelltown, a tiny village at the mouth of the river, least terns rise up from a tottering dock. They dip and soar with the elegance that has earned them the name sea swallows. Through the wide mallow-marshes of silken grasses and satin flowers, they follow us until the river narrows and the forest closes in. Suddenly the terns are gone.

My first glimpse of the other cardinal comes just beyond the city.

This cardinal is a flower, our only red lobelia—so rich a shade the entire plant is often stained with it. It may be a survivor of warm eons before the glacial epoch, for biologists believe that hotter suns than ours made that intense color. The flower's flamboyant hue, brighter even than scarlet, make it a seductive beacon wherever it grows.

It grows sparsely on the Western Shore, but here in the shallows of the Pocomoke it has found an idyllic haven where it may keep its feet wet and its flowers crowned with sunlight. Thus it blooms in stunning profusion well into autumn.

Lush mallows, golden water lilies, jewelweed, blue pickerel-weed and exquisite gypsy clematis share the late-summer scene. All along the river the sweet fragrance of this wild flowing vine hovers over the dusky water. It clambers everywhere amongst the ragged pines trailing lavish garlands of lacy white blossoms as if determined to beautify, single handedly, the entire shoreline.

We spend nearly a week in the upper Pocomoke, dinghying amidst the floating islands of flowers and listening to the lamentations of cicadas. When we reluctantly head home, the trip back down the river is just as idyllic. Amid the cypress knees, flocks of Canada geese talk of autumn, and crimson sparks amid the trees speak of a pending conflagration. Autumn in this vast forest is spectacular.

I recall a line from Thoreau:

How early in the year it begins to be late.

—September 9, 1993

About These Stories

On our Chesapeake travels, we were surprised at the difficulty of accessing the Bay and its many waterways. If you want to get out on the water, you really have to work for it—either you are a commercial fisherman, crabber, or oysterman, or you have the privilege of living along the Bay or own your own watercraft. Much of the Bay's shoreline is private property, developments, or industrial sites, and it's not really all that clear where the public is or is not allowed to enjoy it. Designated state and public parks do provide access at various points but require bringing your own watercraft—a barrier to access for most—and are few and far between, especially given the scale of the Bay. A couple of naturalists we connected with mentioned that people often paddle kayaks to crab houses on the smaller streams and tributaries of the Bay, as many offer launches and docks, and even rentals, as a way to attract customers.

Samantha Pitts, community partnerships coordinator and a teacher naturalist at Pickering Creek Audubon Center in Easton, Maryland, pointed out to us that the center is open from dawn to dusk and provides a place for anyone to launch a kayak or borrow a canoe. She shared with us that some of her favorite moments in the Chesapeake are ones where she realizes that "the water that washes under the dock at Pickering Creek leads out to the Wye River, which leads out to Eastern Bay, and that's directly connected to the Bay," which serves as a nursery for so many wild things. She adds, referring to the cownose rays that come out to the creek to breed in the summer, "If you get in a kayak and they're out, sometimes they'll bump your kayak, which is startling and amazing. The richness of wildlife in the bay and the region—it's something I get pleasure sharing with everybody."

This refreshing piece by Maryland writer Audrey Scharmen— who wrote a regular column for the *Bay Weekly* after she and her husband retired to the Chesapeake Bay from the Southwest—is one of the few water-based stories we could find *not* focused on the industry of the Bay. It conveys a vivid connection to the magic of these beautiful back waterways. We hope it inspires visitors to do the research to get out on the water, and for locals to figure out ways to provide more access.

Chesapeake Crab

CHRISTINE HIGGINS

I marvel at the blue crab
crossing the sand in a stately gait,
no hurry, or so he thinks.
He's moving down the beach,
hauling his verdi gris shell
with his six startling legs of turquoise blue.
The front pincers—for plucking snails
from their shells—are tipped bright red
like new rust. They carry him
back to the water, to his home in the grasses.

All the articulated legs are jointed
like fine jewelry, polished
then washed with a brush stroke of blue.
Last to disappear are his back appendages
shaped at the ends like pumpkin seeds,
filmy white, mother of pearl.

He shines in the morning sun
that rises over the Chesapeake,
where he still reigns as king.

Let's Get Some Crabs

CHRISTINE HIGGINS

I'm not from these parts,
so I had to learn it back then,
when I was newly married—
this particular delight in mounds
of crabs, scalded red and crusted in
Old Bay, dumped onto brown paper
covering any old table.

Our friends and neighbors hoisted
their wooden mallets, ready to strike.
It seemed to me the battle
had already been fought.
Those poor fellows looked up
with beady black eyes, their pincers
no longer moving—defeated.

My new husband taught me how
to pick a crab—turn it over, pull
back the apron, dig out the mustard
with your pinky finger. I learned
to twist the bigger legs into flowers

of luscious meat, moist and flavorful.
Still, not much yield, I thought,
for so much work.

My husband and his friends
sat for hours—picking, sipping beer,
talking. They never got up
from the table. Like a meditation.

I've been here long enough now
to see it's about the gathering,
a ritual that strikes the heart
maybe more than the palette,
the coming together over a couple
dozen crabs, talk that's never heavy—
about the weather, small changes.
Enjoying the fruits of their labor.

About These Stories

It's true that the blue crab "still reigns as king" in the Chesapeake, as Baltimore writer Christine Higgins attests. The scientific name for blue crabs is *Callinectes sapidus*—from the ancient Greek word for "beautiful swimmer" and the Latin word for "savory," a name assigned in 1896 by Dr. Mary J. Rathbun of the Smithsonian, who was among the world's leading experts on crab taxonomy. The underwater native grass beds of the Chesapeake provide an abundant food source for these creatures, who are nourished by the plant matter, mussels, oysters, and crustaceans living here. The beds also shield the crabs from predators and serve as a nursery for juveniles to grow to adulthood. But as these beds disappear due to threats like pollution and warmer waters, so do the blue crabs. Appetite for these tasty crabs has grown at the same time as their population has declined, to the point that the worldwide demand for crab outweighs what the Chesapeake Bay can provide—forcing a lot of Chesapeake crab packing houses to transport and pick crabs caught in North Carolina. Other products advertising "blue crab" or "Maryland-style crab" actually contain crab caught in Asia.

To experience Chesapeake culture, we knew we had to make our way to a crab house. We grabbed a table on the deck with a view of where creek meets cove. With a gaudy interior straight out of the 1980s, the place felt like a kind of church, a central community convening point where the daily service was cracking, peeling, and eating crabs. Except that we were on a schedule, attempting to check off a key experience on our Chesapeake punch card before visiting more maritime museums and libraries before the sun set on a late autumn day. Thinking we'd get a crab cake and move along, we watched as buckets of crabs were dropped on tables covered with brown paper, as diners with wooden mallets pounded on shells and the sweet smell of pulled butter and Old Bay seasoning wafted through the air. Baptized into the house of blue crabs, we decided everything else could wait.

If you're a newbie like us and plan to eat some of these beautiful swimmers, the crab lingo around here can be intimidating. Here's a glossary to help you get started:

Soft-shell crabs. Crabs with a soft, pliable new shell right after shedding their exoskeleton (molting). You can cook and eat soft-shell crabs whole without peeling or picking. Typically available May through September.

Peeler crabs. Crabs before shedding their exoskeleton (molting), with a fully formed soft shell beneath. Often used as bait.

Hard-shell crabs. Crabs with a fully hardened shell. You need to pick the crab meat from this shell. Available April through November.

Jimmy. A male crab, identified by its T-shaped or Washington monument-shaped apron (abdomen).

Sook. A mature female crab, identified by its bell-shaped or Capitol building-shaped apron (abdomen).

Sally. An immature female crab, identified by its triangular apron (abdomen).

Jumbo lump meat. Chunks of meat taken from the large muscles connected to the crab's swimming fins. Tender, with a delicate and sweet flavor.

Backfin meat. Meat from the rear of the crab where the back legs, or "swimmers," are attached. Shredded texture, with a sweet and briny flavor.

Mustard. The organ that filters the crab's blood. Looks yellowish inside a cooked crab. Some eat this but others say you shouldn't, as it contains contaminants.

Dead man's fingers. Gills of the crab. Look spongy and should not be eaten.

Picking the meat from the body of a crab (crab picking) is difficult work. It is typically done by women who have historically worked long hours with no health benefits; in the case of watermen wives, these women take "breaks" only to spend them preparing meals for their husbands who head out to crab at 4:30 a.m., or cleaning, wrapping, and freezing soft-shell crabs. Machines were once invented to automate the picking and cut the labor costs, but the machines left shells in the meat, only proving this is a job for the skilled, hardworking women of the Chesapeake. Environmentalist and journalist Tom Horton praises them in his memoir of life on Smith Island in the Chesapeake, *An Island Out of Time*: "Unless you have picked a crab, armored and spined without, and chambered within by cartilage into more than a dozen tiny, sharp-edged nooks and crannies, you cannot appreciate the speed and skill with which the island pickers transform heaps of the bright orange, steamed hardshells into mounds of glistening white, succulent meat."

We thank those who bring in the crab, for theirs is the good work that allows others to worship at neatly covered tables in crab houses.

Becoming Water: Black Memory in Slavery's Afterlives

MAKSHYA TOLBERT

"I went down to the river to remind myself of the other language."[1]

—JJJJJEROME ELLIS

I was born a few minutes from the Potomac River. Less than a month ago, I packed what I had and headed back to Virginia. I knew some of what I'd find there: oysters, northern water snakes. An array of fish that have made their way through centuries: bass, carp, herring, shad. I knew I'd revisit my family's ghosts, and a river that was once home to a human and more-than-human ecosystem that could ensnare any enslaved Black person seeking safe passage.

Water carries an edge for me, seems to me a dying place. I moved my life from the Potomac River to the Pacific Ocean ten years ago and am just now finding my way back. This time I'm chasing the river, albeit terrified: chasing a lineage of Black watermen, a spillage between my family and the next, a different way of remembering.

I learned not long ago that Black people clung to oysters—a furtive refuge, but an honest one. I learned at that time about Black people's insistence on place. Oystering a cosmology of work, play, and quiet. The cannery, a land of women working for what they could. I thought to myself that oysters must have reminded us of where and to what we belonged. Everything still there, hidden in plain sight.

I'm chasing a river instead of letting the river chase me. This time, I'll live and drift along the Potomac, into the Chesapeake Bay, until I'm on the Atlantic again. As I plan my journey, a line from Martinique-born poet Édouard Glissant ebbs and flows, nudging me: "Do not fear the watery depths."[2]

Why do so many of our crises shape themselves like water? I had run far from the Atlantic: I tried the West Coast, but the hypervigilance of fleeing still seethed through me. I imagined distance itself a refuge; I took myself to a small landlocked town in Northwest Italy and tried to remember who and what I love from there.

In the Mediterranean, another haint awaited me altogether. There, I found another reckoning, another displaced lineage. To leave one crisis was to enter another, or another part of the same. Thousands of refugees taking to water, moving across North Africa and the Mediterranean Sea, many prevented from closing the gap between fleeing and refuge. Everywhere in need of the possibility of flight. By the end of 2019, at least 1,885 people seeking refuge and/or asylum had been claimed by water, most having come from countries excluded from safe, legal processes for seeking asylum. All of their boats, crowded hulls. And then there were the ones that disappeared, *ghost boats* still haunting the waters, whose distress signals went unacknowledged and unanswered. The people on them are believed to have sunk. By the end of 2019, 413 people's lives ended this way: unanswered, left without landings. Less and less seemed possible that year. Refugee boats and slave ships, both stalked by the hold.

Living in Italy drove me to a new point of grief. This is what it is to be haunted by water: you move and the ghosts wear different clothes. I learned how running is always still being chased.

In Bra, an inland *comune* of thirty thousand, I held this mostly alone—though, alone I was not. In the words of Nigerian poet Wale Ayinla, "I write this elegy in the presence of hundreds of ghosts / from my dreams. A strange horizon on a barren sea."[3]

In Bra, I began to find the refuge of language, an anchor with which to steady myself. It was here that Dr. Christina Sharpe's *In the Wake: On Blackness and Being* reintroduced me to the range of the "wake":

> *Wake: the track left on the water's surface by a ship; the disturbance caused by a body swimming or moved, in water; it is the air currents behind a body in flight; a region of disturbed flow. . . .*

> *Wake: a watch or vigil held beside the body of someone who has died, sometimes accompanied by ritual observances including eating and drinking. . . .*

> *Wake: grief, celebration, memory, and those among the living who, through ritual, mourn their passing and celebrate their life in particular the watching of relatives and friends beside the body of the dead person from death to burial and the drinking, feasting, and other observances incidental to this. . . .*

Wake; in the line of recoil of (a gun).

We don't make up ghosts that aren't already adrift.

Sharpe's words slowed some of my internal panic. I began to stay with this feeling that my water fear comes from someplace dark and past and heavy. I heeded Sharpe's insistence on what she calls the "orthography of the wake" and began to fathom her praxis of "wake work": "imagin[ing] new ways to live in the wake of slavery, in slavery's afterlives, to survive (and more) the afterlife of property. . . . a mode of inhabiting and rupturing this episteme with our known lived and un/imaginable lives."[4] My own life patched together pieces of slavery's wake with some hope for a future memory. In Italy, spending as much time with water as my heart allowed, I saw the slave ship, the refugee boat, the Atlantic, the Mediterranean.

I felt undone by water. In Italy, and before, and after. My friends and loved ones sought watering holes and long days on Pacific Ocean beaches. Me? I sought navigational literacy—an ancestral ruttier made of water, night, and stars.

This is what it is to be haunted by water: we become afterlives spilling through our own fingers. Memory refuses to die and shows itself in ripples. Sometimes everything resembles the slave ship. Some nights, a ship out of a beached whale. Some nights, a shipyard of strewn parts. Some nights a shark is a hull, another death. I can conjure a slave ship out of anything.

I don't believe I can leave the slave ship. Bayo Akomolafe tells me it's okay to stay, that the slave ship is "a place of contemplation, as a site of reweaving our connections with grief and loss and trauma and tragedy." I'm drawn to what Akomolafe sees in the slave ship: "a place to sit still, to sit within, to sit with," where "a different sense of freedom can emerge."[5] His words are a steady drip, inviting me to stillness when refuge remains far.

For now, I split myself across the watery depths. Part of me has remained at shore, bridging disasters. In April 2020, no longer in Italy, I accepted a virtual invitation to be with water, in the gesture of holding space for *La Montanña*, a voyage of seven *compañeras* setting sail from Mexico to Europe. The group planned to meet delegates from thirty countries to trade histories of pain, rage, and worldbuilding. I embarked in spirit only.

The rest of me has remained on the slave ship, safety trapped in my ancestral constellation, thousands of ships hoarding stolen life, "the most energetic space in modernity."[6] I think Akomolafe is right: that we never disembarked; that *Clotilda* "reached the American shore, [then] ate the shore . . . became the shore," its entrails carried from the Alabama River into the hinterlands to build ideas of work and order; that we found somewhere to build another ship, another deck, another hold. All of it, a painful mimicry.[7]

I say a prayer of gratitude for the space between water and Black memory, sometimes measured in flight.

In prayer, I find myself at Dunbar Creek on St. Simons Island, Georgia. It is 1803. A story set as much in sky as in water. On the Atlantic, Black people refuse the slavery awaiting them in Georgia. Chained, and "free" of their captors, seventy-five Black people meet a shoal and disembark together. Everything becomes water, including this story. One version retells them walking into the water, singing as they submerge, in chains. Another says they flew up, up, and away—home.

"But what is home if not a floating horizon?"[8] Where is home if not in the breathwork between water and sky? Breathing between water and Black memory, I place language at the shore.

Water decides I will become it.

Water, as it does, reflects. Water becomes a portal, something to sink into or float through. A wild to get lost in as we sing funeral songs, even when no sound comes out. I see how water becomes a life, then becomes a cemetery, then becomes an opening or another life. I pray it true that a future is already dreaming that we swim toward it. What soothes me is Toni Morrison's reflection on water in her talk "The Site of Memory":[9]

> *You know, they straightened out the Mississippi River in places, to make room for houses and livable acreage. Occasionally the river floods these places. "Floods" is the word they use, but in fact it is not flooding; it is remembering. Remembering where it used to be. All water has a perfect memory and is forever trying to get back to where it was.*

With caution, I keep moving toward water. I continue finding water as water seems hell-bent on finding me. Telling me: there are more powerful possibilities than the hold. In tiny and large ways each day—a single droplet of water weighing down a leaf, a walk by a river to cry with—water shows me a sanctuary.

Water continues to be a wild, shapeless place. Somewhere resisting being marked or conquered, try as we will and as I did. So I write poems to heed Glissant's call not to fear the watery depths. I witness how water holds Black memory—and laugh when language arrives late. As vocalist Miho Hatori reflects in her reading of Glissant's poems, "I am learning how to stand between two worlds: the beauty of nature and the darkness of history. Sometimes the rift between them looks endless."[10]

In Virginia, there is water from all angles. Every morning, until the next morning, the water in the air. Nearby, the Atlantic. Nearer by, the Rivanna. From land, what kind of witness of water can I be?

I begin seeing this in all of myself: my work with clay, the poems that want to be made through me, new forms of enchantment that take me *elsewhere*.[11]

In clay, I find another portal, a place to float between "our undoings and our becoming." Working with water and clay, I honor centuries of intuiting with clay, before there was an Atlantic to cross. I hold how the Middle Passage tried to rub all of that away, sink us and our tools into erasure. Clay becomes a portal, a remembering project, a blueprint. A way to transmute violence into healing practice. A way to make the "future in the now."[12]

In one moment, I slip wet clay through my hands and let it take shape between them. My mind reaches for the craftsmanship of David Drake, an enslaved Black potter who made thousands of pots throughout his life while enslaved at Pottersville and across the district of Edgefield, South Carolina. In reaching, I remember Drake's carving on one vessel in particular, on which he inscribed, "I wonder where is all my relations."[13]

And I am always taken back to water. Water becomes a window through which I see myself. So I settle, I float. To float is to anchor myself on water, to find home in what is there. Even if only for a moment. Both heavy and light, I feel the way the poet Christopher Gilbert writes in *Across the Mutual Landscape*: "I reach to touch

/ and the reflection touches me. / Everything is perfect— / even my skin fits."[14]

Floating brings the Atlantic to light, floating allows me the spaciousness of being "the long black language that reaches all the way back."[15] Returning to water itself becomes an attempt toward "wake work," my life itself the site of possibility.

I can barely remember the place I left so long ago, save names and a few dreams. Save my grandmother, whom we buried in Quantico, Virginia, beside the Potomac. Where water is the only salve.

Elsewhere, a person has the grace to ask me, "Are you ready to come back to Virginia?" I consider my courage in quiet possibilities of heading eastward, I imagine riding the Roanoke-bound Amtrak past the Potomac River. I think of spring. Cherry blossoms pink out along the water, and I spot a few budding sugar maples. There are more maples north, fewer where I am headed.

In my notebook, I notice my handwriting leans a bit west. The urge to stay west is stubborn. I am writing down that there are many blues in the sky, it is golden over the river. Ivy chokes almost every tree the train passes by. I think of the trees along the train and the trees along the Potomac. My life is full of channels taking me back to myself.

In her memoir, *Lose Your Mother: A Journey Along the Atlantic Slave Route*, Saidiya Hartman writes: "The country in which you disembark is never the country of which you have dreamed."

I turn to water, welcome the familiar grief, and disembark.

Night Waltz with the Ever Given

can we go
off and steal
the atlantic
        waltz
        to the end
        of the earth
dotted
susurration
blued
        to incoherence
        we become
        undrinkable
water
a frictive
memory
        seething
        containers
        in the night
animal
unable
to swim
        water
        only able
        to swallow
we row wider
irreducible
algae shaped
        a linger
        we become
        a hum
another
ocean
altogether

About This Story

As a border state between the North and South in pre–Civil War America, Virginia embodied an in-between territory. Though *brackish* typically refers to water halfway between salty and fresh, the term could also describe the region's relationship with slavery. By the mid-1800s, free and enslaved Blacks lived side by side throughout the Chesapeake Bay area, but free Blacks were not completely free as long as the specter of slavery hovered over them. A free Black passenger boarding any train might be detained and required to present a certificate proving they were free. Runaway notices were posted in local newspapers offering rewards for escaped slaves. Vigilantes roamed the area, imprisoning and re-enslaving anyone suspected of being an escaped slave, with few consequences for mistaken identity or unjust imprisonment.

In those days, the waterways of the Chesapeake came to represent many things to Black people. Because of the direct access from the Atlantic Ocean, the Chesapeake Bay was where many kidnapped or captured Africans first landed in America to be sold as property. But these same rivers—the Potomac, the Susquehanna, and the smaller tributaries—were integral to the journey toward freedom along the Underground Railroad. For the Black community, water was both a prison and an escape route.

"Brackish" attitudes toward slavery allowed Black workers to learn the oystering trade by working beside White oystermen instead of on a plantation. Newly freed Black watermen were prepared to establish their own oystering businesses just as the oystering industry peaked, offering economic independence.

The legacy of slavery and its connection to water haunts MaKshya Tolbert, a queer writer and poet living "in the ruptures between Black ancestral memory and ecological practice." We appreciate how this story follows Tolbert's journey as they leave their birthplace to outrun the legacy, only to find out that this history is not so easily forgotten. Perhaps we are all learning "how to stand between two worlds: the beauty of nature and the darkness of history."

And still, she beckons

ANNIE MARHEFKA

As a girl, the bay enchanted me: the way your body would ripple like water when bare feet gripped the swaying floor of the boat, the way the other boaters were always smiling and waving their hats at you, the way the fish were plentiful. I loved to watch from the stern as the boat's wake bubbled up into a frothy stream, the shoreline slowly shrinking away.

I remember dropping the line with a flick of the wrist, a finger lifting off the whizzing nylon strand, a satisfying plunk into the bay. I never baited the rods myself, instead watching as my brothers sliced hooks through wriggling worms and wiped boyish hands on t-shirts.

I was desperate to play my part, to fit in with the boys, so I learned to watch the tips of the rods, to tell the difference between the gentle dip of the current tugging and the quick, sharp jerks of a fish nipping at the bait.

We would dip and bob over the waves on the way back to the certainty of the shoreline, counting the fish in our bucket and bickering over who caught which one and how we'd cook them for dinner: grilled over charcoal in the backyard, a sprinkle of seasoning, a lemon squeezed over top the flaky white chunks.

We played *I Spy* with the buoys that marked where crab pots had been dropped. On the bay, they were handmade: a milk jug with holes poked in the sides, a red cloth flag cut from an old shirt. We took naps in the cabin below, our sun-kissed skin hot against the cool sheets.

Now, when my father and I fish, the humidity is relentless, the air capable of drowning you in its thickness. Sometimes you have to dip your face under the water just to breathe.

Instead of buoys, we count houses on the now impermanent shoreline; some days the yards flood and the waterfront in-ground swimming pools are overtaken by the brine of our estuary's tides: freshwater mixed with saltwater mixed with chlorine. No matter how much sand they dredge up to replenish the beaches that serve as front porches for the new homes with too many floors stacked atop foundational stilts, the thirsty bay laps it all back up.

My father is a man of few words but the ones he speaks most often these days are: *I miss your mother, the fish aren't biting*, and *I love you*. We anchor near a sand bar and chum; we drift near the harbor's dry docks and try peelers for bait; we slip bloodworms onto hooks near Pooles Island. Most days, we turn back with empty buckets.

And still, the Chesapeake beckons, the eroding shoreline slipping from her fingertips, her unpredictable churn pulling us in. From her belly, we look back towards the land and she grounds us. Away from the stillness of the shore, she moves beneath us, reminding us she is still here, still breathing, still bleeding.

About This Story

An aspect of the Chesapeake that took us by surprise was the evidence of climate change all around us. It's not coming, it's already here, and many Bay residents have noted severe and sudden changes in their lifetime. We observed pools of water in people's front yards and driveways, and all along roads that parallel or dead end at the Bay, sitting firm with no intention of retreating. We navigated around these pools to walk into museums and drove through them to get to state parks, wondering if the brackish water might bring our car to a halt. Even still, we observed too many beautiful Victorian homes in historic towns along the Bay being rehabbed by contractors—and we wondered, *What for?* Once known for fierce storms and freeze-overs, the Bay is experiencing rapid sea level rise and hot summers, and those who live on the water feel it most acutely.

Taking in sunset from the pier in Crisfield, Maryland, as watermen busily made their way back to the docks, we noticed new high-rise condominiums along the waterfront and recalled a local telling us that Crisfield is a town literally built on top of oyster shells. Is this a sign of optimism for the Bay—or of greed? Many people have been moving into Crisfield, known as the "Crab Capital of the World," with excitement and money, eager to set up shop or settle down before it "takes off." This poem by Annie Marhefka, an author who heads Yellow Arrow Publishing, a Baltimore nonprofit empowering women-identifying writers, demonstrates that this Bay exerts a pull on people, no matter her changing nature, no matter the suffocating heat and empty buckets.

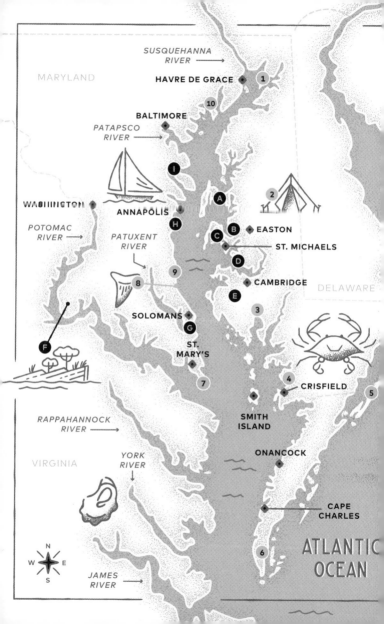

EXPLORE

THE CHESAPEAKE BAY

+

A guide for your next Chesapeake Bay
adventure—on foot or by boat through
the Bay and its tributaries.

ATTRACTIONS

- **A** Chesapeake Bay Environmental Center
- **B** Pickering Creek Audubon Center
- **C** Chesapeake Bay Maritime Museum & Hooper Strait Lighthouse
- **D** Water's Edge Museum
- **E** Harriet Tubman Underground Railroad National Historic Park
- **F** Mallows Bay-Potomac River National Marine Sanctuary
- **G** Calvert Marine Museum
- **H** Annapolis Maritime Museum
- **I** Inner Harbor

NATURAL LANDMARKS

1. Elk Neck State Park
2. Tuckahoe State Park
3. Blackwater Wildlife Refuge
4. Janes Island State Park
5. Assateague/Chincoteague National Seashores
6. Kiptoke State Park
7. Point Lookout State Park and Lighthouse
8. Calvert Cliffs
9. Flags Pond Nature Park
10. Marshy Point Nature Center

What to Do

Beachcomb for prehistoric fossils and shark teeth.

On the western shores of the Chesapeake in southern Maryland, take time to explore the sandy beaches at **Calvert Cliffs State Park** and nearby **Flag Ponds Nature Park**, where you might find prehistoric fossils and shark teeth. The beach at Calvert Cliffs is accessible via a couple of different trails—the more popular Red Trail is 3.6 miles round trip, and the less-traveled, slightly longer Orange Trail is 5 miles round trip. Both trails reward you with stunning views of the cliffs along the Bay, but you should be prepared for trekking through a marsh environment—come dressed for wet, muddy, and buggy trail conditions, including mosquitos and ticks. These cliffs, formed between ten and twenty million years ago when a shallow sea covered what is now southern Maryland, are a geologic marvel that contrast with the otherwise flat and low-lying shorelines and marshes of the region. As the cliffs erode, the bones and teeth of prehistoric sea creatures such as sharks, whales, crocodiles, and massive birds are revealed. From the visitor center area at Flag Ponds Nature Park, a short half-mile hike will get you to another sandy beach on the Bay where you might come across a ten-million-year-old souvenir.

Eat like a local and feast on shellfish . . .

Get ready to crack, slurp, and munch your way through the local cuisine. There is no shortage of crab houses, raw bars, and waterside seafood restaurants where you can enjoy local oysters, rock-fish, scallops, and blue crabs from dock to table.

Enjoy your favorite catch fresh, fried, boiled, broiled, or steamed. Some waterside seafood restaurants now offer ramps and docks so guests can paddle right up to the restaurant. The **Boatyard Bar and Grill** in Annapolis offers nautical flair with seafood staples and specials based on the local catch of the day, or sit riverside and bust out those wood mallets for a crab feast at **Cantler's Riverside Inn**.

Don't leave the Chesapeake without tasting a Smith Island cake, an eight-layer cake whose origin dates back to the 1800s. These cakes were baked by women on Smith Island for their husbands as they shipped off on the autumn oyster harvest, meant to remind the men that they were loved and missed. While traditionally layered with chocolate, the cakes now come in all kinds of flavors—red velvet, vanilla buttercream, cookies and cream, and carrot cake—and can be found in bakeries across the Chesapeake including **Smith Island Baking Company** in Crisfield, Maryland, and **Coastal Baking Company** in Cape Charles, Virginia.

. . . or catch your own supper!

Trying your hand at crabbing, oystering, and fishing is a rewarding and authentic Chesapeake experience that will fill more than just your belly. While catching blue crab used to be much easier before populations declined due to overharvesting and environmental

stressors, there are still areas of the
Chesapeake where they're thriving. For
catching crabs, you will need trotlines,
crab pots, bait, a scoop net to remove crabs
from your trap, a measuring tool to know what you can keep, a
cooler or bucket to store your catch, gloves to protect your hands
from a pinch, and a license.

Oysters can only be harvested commercially or by Maryland
residents recreationally by hand, rake, shaft tong, or diving. You'll
need a bucket to collect them, and since oysters are typically caught
in colder months, you'll also need thick gloves, waders, boots, and
a heavy coat. For fishing, you just need a good ol' rod and
reel—depending on what you're angling to catch. The
Chesapeake is a great region to catch rockfish (striped
bass), speckled trout, white perch, spot, croaker, puppy
drum, catfish, and bluefish. Or, if you'd rather not splurge
on specialized equipment and would like to better your
chances of a good catch, hop aboard a guided chartered
boat with local watermen who take care of all the bait, equipment,
and licensing. An updated list of watermen tours and captains can
be found on the Maryland Office of Tourism's website.

Be mindful of the regulations, guidelines, and best practices for
sustainable harvesting and compliance with local laws, which can be
found on the Maryland Department of Natural Resources website,
in addition to a thoroughly detailed weekly Maryland Fishing Report
that breaks down what people are catching in different regions of
the Bay. If you are on the Virginia side, check the Virginia Marine
Resources Commission website.

Take in Harriet Tubman's route and legacy.

Follow in Harriet Tubman's footsteps along the **Harriet Tubman Underground Railroad Scenic Byway**, which traverses Maryland's Eastern Shore from Cambridge to Goldsboro on beautiful country roads. It's a great way to experience firsthand the secret network of trails, waterways, and safe houses used by enslaved people fleeing northward to freedom. Along the three-to-four-hour drive through Caroline and Dorchester Counties, there are dozens of designated sites where you can stop to appreciate the rich history, culture, and landscapes of this region.

After exploring the **Blackwater National Wildlife Refuge** in Cambridge—dubbed the Everglades of the North—continue down the road to celebrate Harriet's legacy at the **Harriet Tubman Underground Railroad National Visitor Center**, operated jointly by the Maryland Park Service and the National Park Service. Walking trails traverse the 17-acre grounds of the state park. The visitor center includes an exhibit hall featuring multimedia exhibits, a theater, and a gift shop, as well as a large outdoor picnic pavilion. The visitor center building itself is imbued with symbolism and meaning, as the design intentionally frames "a view north, expressing the importance of traveling northward to escape the circumstances of slavery. The space between the buildings grows wider as visitors venture north—a metaphor for freedom—and the view to the south is truncated by the splay of the buildings, suggesting a sense of oppression similar to that associated with the slaveholding states."

Change your perspective—paddle the Bay.

While the Bay covers a massive area and you'll need a car to get around it, there are plenty of ways to spend your day off the roads and see a whole other side of the Chesapeake. The region boasts a number of water trails and ways of recreating that will take you to historic and scenic landscapes accessible only by paddle or sail. If you can BYO watercraft or rent a boat, it's like discovering a portal to a hidden world, adding another dimension to exploring the Chesapeake.

The nation's first all-water National Historic Trail, the **Captain John Smith Chesapeake National Historic Trail**, meanders through the Chesapeake waters and includes popular destinations like the stunning Janes Island State Park. Check out *A Boater's Guide to the Captain John Smith Chesapeake National Historic Trail*, produced by the National Park Service Chesapeake Bay Office in partnership with the Chesapeake Conservancy and the Chesapeake Bay Foundation, available online. It introduces paddlers and boaters to the best places to access the trail.

Janes Island State Park in Crisfield, Maryland, is among the few parks that offer watercraft rentals, and from here you can access 30 miles of water trails and 5 miles of beach accessible only by boat. You can also rent kayaks and paddleboards from the **Chesapeake Bay Environmental Center** in Gransonville, Maryland. Launch right from its dock and enjoy Marshy Creek and the Bay, where you might spot ospreys, eagles, river otters, terrapins, sting rays, waterfowl, and sometimes even dolphins.

For American history buffs, the **Star-Spangled Banner National Historic Trail** is a 560-mile land and water route that runs through Maryland, Virginia, and Washington DC, and traces the history of the Chesapeake Bay, the War of 1812, and, you guessed it, America's national anthem.

If you'd rather peddle than paddle, enjoy the **Cross Island Trail**, a 6.5-mile tree-lined bike path connecting two nature parks on Maryland's Eastern Shore, part of the fifteen-state East Coast Greenway. Along this route, you'll get a glimpse of local neighborhoods, wetlands, inlets, and wildlife (especially ospreys!). If you end your ride in **Terrapin Nature Park**, you can hop off your bike and take a nature trail to the beach for stunning views of the Chesapeake Bay Bridge.

Set sail—board a skipjack, sailboat, or charter.

If you prefer to have somebody else power or steer the boat, you can find private boat tours and charters offered by Chesapeake Bay watermen and waterwomen all across the Bay. These trustworthy guides share the history, heritage, and stories of life on the Bay—from Annapolis to Rock Hall to St. Michaels to Cape Charles. Many maritime museums in the region offer bay and river tours, including the **Annapolis Maritime Museum and Park**, the **Chesapeake Bay Maritime Museum**, and the **Calvert Marine Museum**. Some of the women sailing and chartering boats in the region are highlighted in the Her Helm portrait project, a celebration of women captains in Maryland and Virginia by photographer Kristin Rutkowski.

Stroll along Chesapeake shores and marshes.

In the Uppers, as the locals call it, visit **Marshy Point Nature Center**, which features more than eight miles of hiking trails, two self-guided nature trails, a wildlife observation platform, a butterfly garden, a paddle trail, and a canoe launch and pier. Here you can get an up-close view of more than fifty different native wildlife species, learn about local wildlife through displays and programming, and enjoy the outdoor play space with a skipjack scale model and an eagle's nest. At **Pickering Creek Audubon Center** on the Eastern Shore, you can experience a variety of habitats including mature hardwood forest, fresh and brackish marsh, meadow, tidal and non-tidal wetlands, shorelines, and cropland. This 450-acre working farm and natural habitat on the Eastern Shore of Maryland situated next to the tidal Pickering Creek is a fitting resting place for the cabin of writer Gilbert Byron, who often wrote about these Chesapeake landscapes. If you're headed across the Chesapeake Bay Bridge, stop by the **Chesapeake Bay Environmental Center**, where you will find 510 acres dedicated to environmental education and habitat restoration, a popular destination for birders. Visitors can take self-guided or guided hikes around the pond, climb observation decks, and meander across boardwalks to the bay shores.

Visit maritime museums.

Maritime museums are a *thing* in the Chesapeake. Even if you don't think boats are *your* thing, these museums offer a lot of fascinating information about the history and maritime culture of the region and its landscape. They also provide access to other experiences like lighthouse and boat tours, art exhibitions, and special exhibits and programming.

The **Annapolis Maritime Museum and Park** is a pocket-size museum at the former site of McNasby Oyster Company, the last historic oyster packing plant in the area. The museum features updated technology to give you an immersive experience of the region's history, including a holographic waterman display and a VR view of the interiors of three different kinds of regional boats—plus the museum cat gets bonus points for love and affection. From the rear of the museum, admire the Bay from the dock or buy passes for a variety of skipjack cruises offered. The **Calvert Marine Museum**, beyond sharing maritime history and a tour of Solomon, Maryland's Drum Point Lighthouse, has exhibits on local biology, an outdoor marsh walk, and even resident river otters. For those curious to learn about the region's prehistoric past, it also offers an exhibit about Calvert Cliffs, its geologic history, and the many fossils that have been and can be discovered there.

Our favorite museum was the **Chesapeake Bay Maritime Museum** in St. Michaels, Maryland, where you can easily spend two days taking in the huge campus and range of permanent and rotating special exhibits. Most notable on our visit was the *Oystering on the Chesapeake* exhibit. Visitors can board an interactive skipjack, view a stunning display of the packaging designs of canned oysters, learn about the history of primarily women crab pickers at the *Maryland Crab Meat Company* installation, or climb to the top of the 1879 Hooper Strait Lighthouse. Be sure to check out the **Water's Edge Museum** in Oxford, Maryland, which centers Black farmers, professional sailmakers, military figures, musicians, watermen, and crab pickers through a collection of literature, paintings, lithographs, frescoes, and drawings of African American life in this region.

Visit the Bay's unique lighthouses.

The Chesapeake Bay's shallow and sometimes treacherous waters, complex shorelines, and unpredictable weather often created navigational hazards for mariners, making lighthouses essential for warning them away from shorelines. Now the lights lure visitors with their storied pasts and the chance to view the quarters of the last lighthouse keepers.

The **Thomas Point Shoal Light** in Annapolis is iconic—the only Chesapeake screw-pile lighthouse still in its original location. Screw-pile lighthouses are built on special iron pilings screwed into the muddy bottoms of shallow, dangerous shoals. Another example of this style of lighthouse is the **Hooper Strait Lighthouse** at the Chesapeake Bay Maritime Museum in St. Michaels, Maryland. Here you can stop inside to imagine the solitary and sometimes danger-ous life of the lighthouse keeper—or, to really experience it, check out the museum's Lighthouse Overnight Program for youth and scouting groups, students, and their chaperones to spend the night in the lighthouse.

In the Uppers you can visit the **Turkey Point Lighthouse**, which provides views of beaches, marshes, and wooded bluffs at the Bay's headwaters in North East, Maryland's Elk Neck State Park. Nearby, stop in Havre de Grace to tour the **Concord Point Lighthouse**, the second oldest lighthouse in Maryland. At the mouth of the Potomac River at the bottom western end of the Bay sits the **Point Lookout Lighthouse** in Point Lookout State Park, where a Civil War prison camp confined at its peak more than twenty thousand Confederate soldiers at a time. Legend has it that this lighthouse is haunted.

Visit the Ghost Fleet of Mallows Bay at low tide.

The **Mallows Bay-Potomac River National Marine Sanctuary** is a marine sanctuary designated in 2019 to protect an 18-square mile stretch of the Potomac River where remnants of more than a hundred World War I-era wooden steamships—known as the Ghost Fleet—lie in the bed of the river. This is the site where the ships ended up after being picked apart for scrap, and now a century later they serve an ecologically valuable purpose as intertidal habitats for fish, beavers, osprey, blue heron, and bald eagles. You can see the ships emerge from the water at low tide, an ideal time to paddle out and explore these relics. The sanctuary also has walking trails that feature signage educating visitors about the Piscataway people native to this land.

Use your binoculars to check out the birds.

The marshes and shorelines of the Chesapeake, which rests along a critical migratory route in the Atlantic Flyway, make this region a bird lover's paradise. The tidal marshes, shorelines, and other wetlands in the Chesapeake are an ideal habitat for the more than four hundred bird species and thirty different waterfowl species that utilize this flyway to feed, breed, and nest. Here you can spot a diverse range of bird and waterfowl species, including osprey, bald eagles, great blue herons, geese, swans, mallards, screech owls, pileated woodpeckers, pelicans, red-winged blackbirds, egrets, ibises, and terns. Excellent locations for bird-watching include the **Blackwater National Wildlife Refuge, Pickering Creek Audubon Center,** and the **Eastern Neck National Wildlife Refuge.**

If you're visiting in the winter, you may witness the spectacle of hundreds of thousands of migrating snow geese arriving from their summer breeding grounds in the Arctic, gathering or taking flight from the Eastern Shore. Their presence is a full sensory experience that includes the almost ominous shadow of their arrival blocking the sun, the sight of marshes and fields blanketed in white, and the deafening chorus of squawks and honks and thumping wings as they depart.

Bald eagles can be seen year-round and are not only the symbol of our country but also an environmental success story. The use of DDT landed eagles on the endangered species list. After the chemical was banned, the Chesapeake region played a very important role in their population rising, as eagles found success in breeding and raising healthy eaglets at the **Blackwater National Wildlife Refuge**. Head over to **Conowingo Dam** on the Susquehanna River to increase your chances of spotting an eagle, as the base of the dam is a favorite source of fish for these incredible birds.

One caution: when setting out on a hike or bird-watching expedition, avoid designated hunting areas during hunting season. Hunting, and especially waterfowl hunting, is a beloved tradition and popular source of sustenance in the Bay region.

Visit the barrier islands.

While it's easy to spend several days just exploring the Bay, nearby **Assateague and Chincoteague Islands** off Virginia's Eastern Shore are worth making time for. The biodiversity and characteristics of the Virginia barrier islands are fascinating and dynamic—shifting with the tides, winds, and force of the Atlantic Ocean. Both islands are known for the ponies that roam freely and have made these barrier beaches home. While extremely adorable, these ponies are wild animals, so they will not be giving rides anytime soon. Their origin story is legendary—they've adapted to the island ecosystem of marshes, dunes, and woodlands over the course of many centuries. The annual Chincoteague Pony Swim at the end of July, when wild ponies from Assateague Island make a swim across the channel to Chincoteague guided by volunteer firefighters, is part of a larger penning event intended to manage the size of the herd to protect its health and sustainability as well as the ecosystem.

The **Assateague Island National Seashore and the Chincoteague National Wildlife Refuge** are extraordinary pristine shorelines along the Atlantic Ocean where you can explore sandy beaches, salt marshes, maritime forests, and coastal bays. Many months of the year can be quite buggy, sun exposed, and windy, so if you are planning to spend time outdoors, be sure to pack accordingly. Visit the gateway town of **Berlin, Maryland**, another charming downtown with shops, restaurants, and antique shops. Berlin's hidden gem is the **Mermaid Museum**, a small and quirky place dedicated to the lore of mermaids, offering lots of photo and dress-up opportunities. Don't miss the mermaid-shaped Cheeto on display.

At the other end of Virginia's Eastern Shore, stop at the scenic lookout points along the **Chesapeake Bay Bridge Tunnel**. Crossing over and under the mouth of Chesapeake Bay, the 17.6-mile bridge-tunnel connects the Eastern Shore to mainland Virginia and is considered an engineering marvel.

How to Visit Well

Volunteer to help protect the Bay.

An impressive number of nonprofits, foundations, and alliances work together on efforts to conserve, restore, protect, advocate for, and educate people about the Chesapeake. Because the Bay is so massive and has tributaries running through six states, it takes an all-hands-in effort to protect its biodiversity, improve its water quality, and lessen human impact on its ability to thrive. Many of these efforts focus on restoring habitat, planting trees and native vegetation, building and seeding oyster reefs, monitoring water quality, advocating for policy, organizing volunteer cleanup events, surveying wildlife, raising awareness, and educating residents on small changes with big impact.

Trees play an important part in maintaining the health of the Bay by providing habitats that support the diverse native wildlife of the region and slowing down or filtering pollutants in rainwater before it reaches the Bay. There are many ways to support efforts to plant trees, including volunteering with organizations. Some of our favorites include Anacostia Riverkeeper, the Alliance for the Chesapeake Bay, the Chesapeake Bay Foundation, the Chesapeake Bay Trust, the Chesapeake Conservancy, the Chesapeake Legal Alliance, the Chesapeake Oyster Alliance, the Eastern Shore

Land Conservancy, the Maryland Coastal Bays Program, the Oyster Recovery Partnership, ShoreRivers, and Waterkeepers Chesapeake. You don't need to join an organized effort, either—if you're enjoying time along the Bay's shores, consider packing a trash bag to clean up litter you spot.

Support organizations telling an inclusive Bay story.

This watershed is dependent on collective action to save the Bay, and this spirit carries through in the efforts of those who work to preserve and give voice to the diverse backgrounds, cultures, races, ethnicities, and identities in the region. Given that 8 percent of the residents of the Chesapeake Bay watershed are Hispanic and Latino, two organizations have mobilized to serve them: Corazón Latino, which partners with the National Park Service to engage these communities through culturally relevant and linguistically appropriate experiences within the NPS Chesapeake Gateways and Watertrails Network; and Defensores de la Cuenca (Watershed Defenders), a Latino-led nonprofit dedicated to connecting this community to nature through shared experiences and opportunities to preserve and defend the Chesapeake Bay watershed.

The Blacks of the Chesapeake Foundation preserves the legacy of the Black watermen and farmers of this area through programming, education, heritage tourism training, and publications about their history. The Water's Edge Museum seeks to empower the young people of today to find their place in history by highlighting the lives of Black farmers, professional sailmakers, military figures, musicians, watermen, and crab pickers. Minorities in Aquaculture educates women of color on the environmental benefits of aquaculture and supports them in their careers in the field, growing the seafood industry and creating an empowering space for women. Annapolis

Queer Outdoors and the Venture Out Project are two organizations offering events and hikes for the LGBTQ+ community.

The Accokeek Foundation partners with the National Park Service to enhance the visitor experience at Piscataway Park, where it provides programming and services to share the historical and cultural significance and regenerative potential in the interconnectedness of nature, agriculture, cultural history, and foodways on this landscape. You can also support nonprofits like the Chesapeake Conservancy that fund and work in partnership on initiatives like the Rappahannock Tribe's Return to the River. This initiative has worked to restore Fones Cliffs, a sacred site, to the tribe. A permanent conservation easement of 465 acres at the cliffs, now renamed Pissacoake, will be used by the tribe to create trails and a replica of a sixteenth-century village, where the tribe can educate the public about its history and Indigenous approaches to conservation as well as connect future generations of Rappahannock youth to their tribal traditions and the Rappahannock River.

Follow all fishing, crabbing, and hunting rules.

If you intend to go fishing, crabbing, or hunting on the Bay, it's important to be aware of the local rules when you go. Licenses, permits, fees, and regulations are put in place to limit when and what you catch or shoot to ensure a sustainable future for wildlife. Check the websites of these agencies before you go: the Maryland Department of Natural Resources, the Virginia Department of Wildlife Resources, the Virginia Marine Resources Commission, and the US Fish and Wildlife Service.

When you're out on the water, secure items on your watercraft so they don't blow overboard and retrieve anything that does. Be particularly mindful of items that harm wildlife like fishing line and hooks, plastic bags and single-serve wrappers, and bottles and cans. Follow the "pack it in, pack it out" rule and dispose of these items at home. Handle marine waste appropriately, keep motorboat engines well tuned, and refill fuel tanks on shore to avoid leaking contaminants into the water.

Practice "careful catch and release" by keeping only the fish you're going to use and letting the rest go to conserve the Bay's resources. Even if you are only catching to release, it's important to follow guidelines to ensure fishes' survival once released: do not remove the fish from the water, use circle hooks and dehooking devices, and reduce the fight time. If you're bringing your own watercraft and gear—like waders, boots, kayaks, canoes, motorboats, and boat trailers—be sure to thoroughly empty sitting water and wash them to avoid spreading invasive plants or critters in the water or your next destination.

Buy local.

Strict state and federal fishing regulations ensure that commercial fishermen in the region are harvesting and conducting business responsibly and sustainably. You get to help by *eating* it! Buying fresh, high-quality seafood cultivated and harvested in the Chesapeake Bay means you're supporting local watermen, their families, and the local economy—the people invested in clean waters and rebounding populations—and thereby ensuring the future of this ecosystem. Buying from local farms is another way to support the local economy, cut down on transportation emissions, and reduce air pollution—among the biggest contributors to nitrogen pollution in the Bay.

Beyond food, shopping locally in the charming small towns across the Bay is a fun way to support the local economy *and* take some authentic Chesapeake home with you. The region boasts creative and quirky shops with locally made products in towns like Annapolis, Chestertown, Cambridge, Chesapeake City, Easton, St. Michaels, Cape Charles, and Onancock. The Torpedo Factory Art Center along the Potomac River in Alexandria, Virginia, is a former munitions plant now home to the nation's largest collection of working artists' open studios. Here you can pick up handmade goods from more than seventy artists working in media including painting, ceramics, photography, jewelry, stained glass, fiber, printmaking, and sculpture.

Donate shells.

Planning to eat a lot of oysters on your travels? Oyster shells are the best natural resource for rebuilding reefs and are in short supply, so there are many efforts to involve residents in saving discarded shells to reuse in oyster restoration projects. You can take part, too. Be sure to eat at restaurants or festivals across Maryland, Virginia, and DC partnering with the Oyster Recovery Partnership's Shell Recycling Alliance and the Chesapeake Bay Foundation's Save Oyster Shells programs—or you can drop off your shells if cooking at your campsite or rental.

Consider where you stay.

One way to support the local community in the Chesapeake Bay is opting for local and historic hotels, motels, and bed-and-breakfast inns instead of chains. The Bay's small towns offer locally owned accommodations in an array of historic buildings, former mansions, Victorian homes, and townhouses, each with its own unique character and the maritime feel of the Chesapeake. If you are booking through platforms like Airbnb or VRBO, take the extra time to read the property listing or host's bio to see what they might be doing to support the community and environment around them. For example, look for listings that indicate a BayScaped yard—favoring native plants instead of exotics that need fertilizers that in turn can pollute the waters—or accommodations that offer bikes, boats, or composting for guests.

Use only local firewood.

All visitors can play a role in keeping the Chesapeake forests safe from invasive pests that kill trees, like the emerald ash borer and other invasive beetles. Avoid using untreated firewood from outside of the region and instead buy local firewood provided by the campgrounds and state parks.

Towns to Visit

The Chesapeake Bay is lined with quaint historic small towns offering restaurants, boutique shops, art galleries, bookstores, cafes, and museums. On the western shore of the Bay you have two of the Chesapeake's biggest cities. Baltimore sits at the helm with a bustling inner harbor, impressive museums, and nightlife. Annapolis, less than an hour south, is a true gem of the Chesapeake with a lively cultural and dining scene. Just northeast of Baltimore, Havre de Grace sits at the mouth of the Susquehanna River where it meets the Bay a stunning waterfront along a historic downtown. On the Eastern Shore in Maryland, a plethora of charming small towns are worth a visit, including Cambridge, Chestertown, Crisfield ("the Crab Capital of the World"), Easton, Oxford, Rock Hall, and St. Michaels. On the Virginia side, you'll want to stop by the equally charming towns of Cape Charles and Onancock.

Annapolis, sitting along the west side of the Bay, was briefly the capital of the United States and is now the capital of Maryland and unofficially "the Sailing Capital of the US." A historic town with maritime charm, Annapolis is known for its colonial architecture and eighteenth-century brick buildings. Its brick streets and buildings along with its warm lights give it a romantic glow any night of the year, but especially in winter when the sailboats are alight for the holidays. The town is bustling with seafood restaurants, shops, ice cream parlors, and scenic views of the Bay along its waterfront, and is home to the US Naval Academy and St. John's College. Ego Alley in the heart of Annapolis is where people go to show off or gawk at boats.

Cambridge is located in Dorchester County, Maryland, on the eastern shore of the Bay along the Choptank River. This region is heavily associated with Harriet Tubman's legacy, and Cambridge is the perfect town to grab a meal before visiting the Harriet Tubman Underground Railroad Visitor Center. Its downtown offers restaurants, art galleries, public art, bookstores, and boutique shops, and also hosts a number of art walks, parades, and community events.

Sitting on a small peninsula surrounded by the Bay on Virginia's Eastern Shore, **Cape Charles** is a cute historic beach town with turn-of-the-century architecture, Victorian homes, boutique stores, restaurants, coffee shops, a bookstore, a brewery, and art galleries just steps away from the beach and fishing piers. Be sure to visit the nearby Kiptopeke State Park, and don't forget to take a selfie at the LOVEwork sculpture along the pier at the public beach, one of three hundred beloved LOVEworks across Virginia, each reflecting its location's unique history and community.

Nestled along Maryland's Chesapeake and Delaware Canal, **Chesapeake City,** is listed on the National Register of Historic Places. The town maintains its historic charm through its nineteenth-century architecture and is a favorite weekend getaway for its waterfront restaurants, shops, bike trails, and outdoor concerts in the summer months. Visit the C&D Canal Museum to take in the history of the canal, ships, steam engines, and bridges.

Easton was founded in 1790 and has a historic downtown lined with antique stores, upscale boutiques, art galleries, cafes, shops, restaurants, historic inns, and the Academy Art Museum. It often ranks on Best Small Towns of America lists and prides itself as the cultural capital of the Eastern Shore. Be sure to stop by the Frederick Douglass statue at the courthouse, the site of his "Self-Made Men" speech to a segregated audience. Each year Easton hosts the Waterfowl Festival, a quintessential Chesapeake event, bringing thousands of people to the Eastern Shore to celebrate the region's sporting and hunting heritage. It is also home to Plein Air Easton, the largest juried plein air painting competition in the US.

At the headwaters of the Bay where the Susquehanna River flows in sits **Havre de Grace,** a charming small town with shops, antique stores, restaurants, and museums. The Havre de Grace Decoy Museum houses an extensive collection of working and decorative Chesapeake Bay decoys, once commonly used to lure waterfowl within range of a hunter's shotgun. Visit the scenic Havre de Grace Promenade to see the Concord Point Lighthouse, stroll along the boardwalks, and stop by the Havre de Grace Maritime Museum. Bird lovers might enjoy the carved wooden birds atop the dock pilings at the Concord Point Pier, where you can catch a serene view of the water. Antique lovers will delight in Seneca Cannery Antiques, filled wall to wall with previously loved goods across three floors, many with a Chesapeake flair.

One of the oldest towns in Virginia, founded in 1680 and trade center of the Eastern Shore for 250 years, **Onancock** is now a bustling artisan community called the "Coolest Town in the South." It was once described as "the Gem of the Eastern Shore" by Captain

John Smith, and once you get out on the water and take in the unparalleled views of land and wildlife, you'll see why. Onancock has award-winning restaurants, a winery, a 1950s movie theater, art galleries, museums, and live theater. From spring through fall you can catch a ferry or a sailboat to Tangier Island, a unique place with a tiny population, few cars, and its own dialect.

St. Michaels is a beloved waterfront town situated on Maryland's Miles River where it meets the Chesapeake Bay. Talbot Street offers a brewery, a winery, a distillery, restaurants, and boutique shops. The Chesapeake Bay Maritime Museum is a must-visit, and admission gets you two days to explore its extensive collection and campus. You'll need it!

Where to Camp

Elk Neck State Park, along the headwaters of the Chesapeake Bay in Maryland. Features a quiet, peaceful, and private campground offering a range of activities, including hiking out to the Turkey Point Lighthouse, kayak rentals, fishing, and bird-watching, and with a playground. It's also close enough for day trips to Baltimore, Chesapeake City, and Havre de Grace.

Janes Island State Park, on the Bay's Eastern Shore near Crisfield, Maryland—"the Crab Capital of the World." While most of this state park is to be explored by watercraft, the campground itself is set in a stunning stand of tall pine trees right along the Bay. The camping area offers a variety of sites and cabins, a lodge, a camp store and nature center, boat ramps, and a marina—and you can even store your RV here for the season!

Kiptopeke State Park, on Virginia's Eastern Shore. The stunning dog- and kid-friendly campground offers a range of sites, cabins, yurts, a bunkhouse, and lodges with beach access. Don't forget your bike, kayak, or fishing gear. This state park has boardwalk trails for hiking, a fishing pier, and small beachfronts to watch incredible sunsets and ships out on the water. While you're here, visit the charming nearby town of Cape Charles.

Susquehanna State Park, along the Susquehanna River at the headwaters of the Chesapeake Bay in Maryland. Popular for biking, hiking, and fishing. The campground, with heavy forest cover, offers standard amenities, a camp store, a playground, hiking trails, and park programming about local wildlife.

Tuckahoe State Park, a local favorite in Queen Anne, Maryland, on the eastern side of the Bay. The pet-friendly campground offers cabins and tent sites with standard camp amenities and a camp store, a boathouse, disc golf, a tire playground, and volleyball courts. Set along woodlands, the park has a 60-acre lake and creek for paddling or fishing, 15 miles of multiuse trails, and family activities in the summer months.

In addition to these public campgrounds, you can also arrange campsites through camping companies, such as Hipcamp, that provide access to private land and campsites while supporting local communities and preserving natural spaces.

Community Resources

Accokeek Foundation partners with the National Park Service to manage Piscataway Park, the tribal homeland of the Piscataway people. The foundation seeks to honor the Indigenous people by sharing the cultural history of the Piscataway, offering trail access and farm tours, and telling the evolving stories about different communities' reliance on the land for sustenance.

accokeek.org

Alliance for the Chesapeake Bay collaborates with individuals and organizations to restore the lands and waters of the Bay's watershed. Through programs focused on forests, agriculture, green infrastructure, and stewardship and engagement, the alliance positions itself to prevent pollution where it begins—on the land—before it reaches the rivers and the Bay.

allianceforthebay.org

Blacks of the Chesapeake Foundation is a nonprofit that seeks to document and preserve the history of African Americans who have worked in the maritime and seafood industries of the Chesapeake Bay. Led by its founder and president, Vincent O. Leggett, the foundation offers a broad range of historical, cultural, and educational activities.

blacksofthechesapeake.wildapricot.org

Chesapeake Beaches Blog records Jody Couser's quest to visit as many sandy beaches as she can along the Chesapeake. This pandemic project turned into a multiyear pursuit that has provided a ton of helpful information about more than a hundred beaches to those wanting to explore public access to the Chesapeake.
chesapeakebeaches.weebly.com

Chesapeake Conservancy is a nonprofit based in Annapolis, Maryland, that uses technology to enhance the pace and quality of conservation, and help build parks, trails, and public access sites. This team of conservation entrepreneurs believes the Chesapeake is a national treasure that should be accessible to everyone and a place where wildlife can thrive.
chesapeakeconservancy.org

Chesapeake Oyster Alliance is a coalition of nonprofits, community organizations, oyster growers, and others that aims to add ten billion oysters to the Bay by 2025 by emphasizing the economic benefits and engaging new constituencies. The alliance is driven by the realization that restoring the Bay is only possible if it has a healthy oyster population.
chesapeakeoysteralliance.org

Defensores de la Cuenca connects members of the Latino community to the Chesapeake watershed and each other. The Latino-led nonprofit offers shared experiences and opportunities to preserve and defend the watershed for healthier minds, bodies, and souls.
defensoresdelacuenca.org

Eastern Shore Land Conservancy is nonprofit dedicated to conserving, stewarding, and advocating for the unique rural landscape of Maryland's Eastern Shore. It promotes land conservation and planning to provide public access to Chesapeake Bay and surrounding lands, as well as helping towns become models of innovative economic development and resilience in the face of climate change.
eslc.org

Her Helm is a portrait project founded by photographer Kristin Rutkowski to celebrate women making their own way on the water. The project is dedicated to sharing the inspiring stories of female captains, documenting their backgrounds and experiences, and honoring for their resilience and determination in forging their path in the maritime world.
herhelm.com

Marshy Point Nature Center, on the Chesapeake waterfront in Baltimore County, offers interactive exhibits and innovative programs to engage people of all ages in meaningful and educational outdoor experiences.
marshypoint.org

Minorities in Aquaculture is a nonprofit dedicated to supporting women of color in building careers in aquaculture. The organization aims to create a more inclusive and diverse industry by educating this underrepresented group about the environmental benefits that aquaculture provides and offering career development opportunities to minority women.
mianpo.org

Oyster Recovery Partnership is a nonprofit expert in Chesapeake Bay oyster restoration. The organization is restoring the Bay's native oyster population by building sanctuary reefs, rebuilding public fishery reefs, supporting the aquaculture (oyster farming) industry, recycling oyster shells, and engaging the public through hands-on volunteering and events.
oysterrecovery.org

Pickering Creek Audubon Center is a sanctuary dedicated to conserving natural habitats on Maryland's Eastern Shore. In addition to offering nature programs for schools, teachers, and junior naturalists, the center invites anyone to explore 120 acres of restored nontidal wetland, 100 acres of hardwood forest, and more than 4 miles of trails. It provides water access for launching paddle boats and preserves the cabin of Chesapeake writer Gilbert Byron.
pickeringcreek.org

United4CNRA is a coalition of organizations and individuals led by the Chesapeake Conservancy to advocate for a Chesapeake National Recreation Area (CNRA). The CNRA would be a collection of new and existing parks highlighting the Bay across Maryland and Virginia. It would leverage the resources of the National Park Service to improve public access to the Bay, share its untold stories, and protect the natural environment.
united4cnra.com

Waterkeepers Chesapeake is part of the worldwide Waterkeeper Alliance fighting for swimmable, fishable, drinkable waterways. It promotes grassroots advocacy by supporting waterkeepers throughout the Chesapeake and coastal regions as they protect their communities, rivers, and streams from pollution.

waterkeeperschesapeake.org

Water's Edge Museum in Oxford, Maryland, offers a collection of literature, paintings, lithographs, frescoes, and drawings of African American life in the Chesapeake region. It highlights Black farmers, professional sailmakers, military figures, musicians, watermen, and crab pickers to inspire and empower their descendants.

watersedgemuseum.org

Essential Reads

Salt Tide: Currents of Nature and Life on the Virginia Coast
by Curtis J. Badger (Countryman Press, 1999)

Gilbert Byron: Selected Poems (Literary House Press, 1993)

**An Island Out of Time: A Memoir of
Smith Island in the Chesapeake**
by Tom Horton (W.W. Norton, 2008)

Chesapeake
by James A. Michener (Random House, 1978)

**Night Flyer: Harriet Tubman and
the Faith Dreams of a Free People**
by Tiya Miles (Penguin, 2024)

Arpeggio of Redwings: Chesapeake Seasons: A Guide to Joy
by Audrey Y. Scharmen (New Bay Books, 2020)

**Chesapeake Requiem: A Year with the
Watermen of Vanishing Tangier Island**
by Earl Swift (Dey Street, 2008)

Beautiful Swimmers: Watermen, Crabs and the Chesapeake Bay
by William W. Warner (Back Bay Books, 1994)

Skipjack: The Story of America's Last Sailing Oystermen
by Christopher White (St. Martin's Press, 2009)

A Boater's Guide to the Captain John Smith Chesapeake National Historic Trail
by John Page Williams (National Park Service Chesapeake Bay Office, 2011)

Acknowledgments

Working on this book series as parents to two young kids has required a village. Ilyssa, first and foremost, would like to thank Dave for supporting and encouraging her enthusiasm for this new *Campfire Stories* series and her decision to not plow right into a new job. With Ilyssa taking the lead on travel to research these books, Dave took on the primary responsibility for cooking every meal, doing every drop-off and pickup for two kids at two different schools, conducting the bedtime routine *every night*, and generally keeping our kids alive, full of snacks, and happy—often for a week at a time. Without Dave's unwavering belief in Ilyssa's passion and ideas, in addition to his editing and writing contributions, there would be no *Campfire Stories*. We'd also like to thank Ilyssa's mom, Diane Shapiro, who supports us during these times of travel and writing—and our many friends who host the girls for playdates and sleepovers.

We'd also like to thank our daughters, Lula and Isla, for inspiring us to pursue our passions and for their patience and understanding when we have to travel—even when it makes them feel *like a barnacle drifting all alone at sea*.

We are so grateful to Kate Rogers, editor in chief of Mountaineers Books, who curiously continues to entertain our *many* ideas, and—with honesty and great wisdom—helps to refine and shepherd them into the world. We extend this appreciation to the rest of the Mountaineers Books team, whose enthusiasm for our projects is deeply felt—and with a special shout out to Joleen Simmons, who makes us feel like rock stars. To our editing team, Beth Jusino and Lorraine Anderson—we are grateful for your meticulous editorial work, and we admire your ability to take on a massive collection of stories spanning many centuries with enthusiasm and patience.

This series would not be what it is without Melissa McFeeeters, who has been with us from the very beginning and has designed all of our *Campfire Stories* projects—likely the reason you, reader, picked up our book in the first place!

We'd also like to thank the writers, librarians, researchers, and staff and/or volunteers at the many nonprofit organizations and museums we've connected with across the Chesapeake Bay for your generosity and time. Our understanding of these places without your personal stories, lived experiences and history, and special connections to them would be far less authentic, passionate, and informed. We'd especially like to thank Jody Couser of the Chesapeake Conservancy, who offered invaluable insights about the Bay and connections to others doing important work to protect it. We'd also like to thank Kate Fritz and Adam Miller of the Alliance for the Bay; John Lehman and Nina Jay from the Marshy Point Nature Center; and Samantha Pitts at Pickering Creek Audubon Center—all of whom shared their time and passion for the Bay with us.

To the bookstore buyers and staff who take time to chat with us while we're on our research trips, who educate us on local writers and important literature as well as carve a little space on your shelves for our book or feature it in your beautiful, creative displays—we see you and we appreciate you. We can't express how delighted we are to receive texts from friends and family traveling across the US who spot our books or card decks in the wild, or when we ourselves encounter them in real life. It never gets old.

Last, to our dear readers whose insatiable desire for stories from our wild places allows us to continue collecting stories—we are grateful for your curiosity, love for our natural world, and desire to follow in the age-old tradition of storytelling. Without those readers who reached out or attended our events to say, *When are you going to do MY favorite place in the world?* or challenged us to consider places outside of national parks, we wouldn't have this new series.

Notes

"Harriet Tubman, Woodswoman" by Tiya Miles

1. Lois E. Horton, *Harriet Tubman and the Fight for Freedom: A Brief History with Documents* (Boston: Bedford / St. Martin's, 2013), v.

2. Judy Bryant, Oral Interview Project, Maryland State Parks, November 18, 2011. The year before Tubman died, Judy Bryant's family planted two trees to mark the graves of Tubman's brother (William Henry Ross Stewart, Sr.), nephew (William H. Stewart, Jr.), and niece-in-law (Emma Moseby Stewart). The baby trees grew together over time, creating the largest tree in the cemetery. Tubman was buried near her relatives and the memorial trees, a fitting symbol of her life and the value she placed on relationality and interconnection. Kate Larson email to Tiya Miles, July 16, 2023.

3. Dorceta E. Taylor, *The Rise of the American Conservation Movement* (Durham, NC: Duke University Press, 2016), loc. 2707, Kindle.

4. Emma P. Telford, "Harriet: The Modern Moses of Heroism and Visions," unpublished, c. 1905, in the collection of the Cayuga Museum of History and Art, Auburn, New York, 6.

5. Sarah H. Bradford, *Harriet: The Moses of Her People* (G. R. Lockwood and Son, 1886; digital version available from Smithsonian Libraries: library.si.edu/digital-library/book/harrietmosesofhoobrad), 22.

6. Benjamin Drew, *The Narratives of Fugitive Slaves in Canada* (Boston: John P. Jewett and Company, 1856), 30.

7. Kate Clifford Larson, *Bound for the Promised Land: Harriet Tubman, Portrait of an American Hero* (New York: One World / Ballantine Books, 2004), 56.

8. Janell Hobson, "Karen V. Hill, Director of the Harriet Tubman Home: 'She Was Able to Separate the Brutality of Slavery from How She Loved the Land,'" *Ms.* magazine, March 2, 2022, 3.

9. Ednah Dow Cheney, "Moses," *Freedmen's Record*, March 1865, reprinted in Lois E. Horton, *Harriet Tubman and the Fight for Freedom: A Brief History with Documents* (Boston: Bedford / St. Martins, 2013), 135.

10. Catherine Clinton, *Harriet Tubman: The Road to Freedom* (New York: Back Bay Books, 2004), 20.

11. Larson, *Bound*, 58. Michael E. Ruane, "Harriet Tubman's Lost Maryland Home Found, Archaeologists Say," *Washington Post*, April 20, 2021.

12. Bradford, *Harriet*, 111.

13. Larson quote in Ruane, "Harriet Tubman's Lost Maryland Home," *Washington Post*.

14. Taylor, *Rise*.

15. Telford, "Harriet," 6.

16. Allison Keyes, "Harriet Tubman, an Unsung Naturalist, Used Owl Calls as a Signal on the Underground Railroad," *Audubon Magazine*, February 25, 2020.

17. Kimberly N. Ruffin, *Black on Earth: African American Ecoliterary Traditions* (Athens, GA: University of Georgia Press, 2010), 72.

18. Crenshaw quote in Keyes, "Harriet Tubman."

"Becoming Water: Black Memory in Slavery's Afterlives" by MaKshya Tolbert

1. JJJJJerome Ellis, "Bend Back the Bow and Let the Hymn Fly," *The Clearing* (New York: Wendy's Subway, 2021).

2. Édouard Glissant, *The Collected Poems of Édouard Glissant*, trans. Jeff Humphries and Melissa Manolas (Minneapolis: University of Minnesota Press, 2019).

3. Wale Ayinla, "Chronicles of Strangers in Dialogue (A Survivor's Testament)" in *To Cast a Dream* (Miami: Jai-Alai Books, 2021).

4. Christina Sharpe, *In the Wake: On Blackness and Being* (Durham, NC: Duke University Press, 2016).

5. Bayo Akomolafe, "Let Us Make Sanctuary," Sep 30, 2020, Sounds True, www.youtube.com/watch?v=m4XkmPxpogI.

6. Bayo Akomolafe, "The Destruction of Earth and the Exploitation of People," Facebook, April 22, 2021, www.facebook.com/watch/?v=814596539474111.

7. Akomolafe, "Destruction."

8. Cherise Morris, from the essay "the cosmic matter of Black lives," originally published in *The Iowa Review*, Volume 48, Issue 2.

9. From Toni Morrison's "The Site of Memory," a talk published in *Inventing the Truth: The Art and Craft of Memoir*, 2d ed., ed. William Zinsser (New York: Houghton Mifflin, 1995).

10. Miho Hatori, "Édouard Glissant's *Sun of Consciousness*," *Bomb*, March 12, 2020, bombmagazine.org/articles/%C3%A9douard-glissants-sun-of-consciousness.

11. In his book *Begin Again: James Baldwin's America and Its Urgent Lessons for Our Own* (New York: Crown, 2021), Eddie S. Glaude Jr. describes "elsewhere" as "that physical or metaphorical place that affords the space to breathe."

12. Saidiya Hartman in "Poetry Is Not a Luxury: The Poetics of Abolition," a panel discussion with Saidiya Hartman, Canisia Lubrin, Nat Raha, and Christina Sharpe, along with Nydia A. Swaby as chair, August 10, 2020, silverpress.org/blogs/news/poetry-is-not-a-luxury-the-poetics-of-abolition.

13. *I Made This Jar: The Life and Works of the Enslaved African-American Potter, Dave*, ed. Jill Beute Koverman (Columbia: McKissick Museum, University of South Carolina, 1998).

14. Christopher Gilbert, "Now," *Across the Mutual Landscape* (Minneapolis: Graywolf Press, 1984).

15. Christopher Gilbert, "Horizontal Cosmology," *Across the Mutual Landscape* (Minneapolis: Graywolf Press, 1984).

Permissions
and Sources

Payne, Lara. "Estuary, the Chesapeake Bay." Printed with the permission of the author.

RagghiRain. "Creation of Toolup Ahkiy." Printed with the permission of the author.

Scharmen, Audrey Y. "Autumn Sharpens Our Senses" and "Elegy for a Chesapeake Fish House." Printed with the permission of the author.

Shomette, Donald Gary. "Ghost Fleet of Mallow's Bay." Printed with the permission of the author.

Tolbert, MaKshya. "Becoming Water." Printed with the permission of the author.

Warner, William W. "The Bay." From *Beautiful Swimmers* by William W Warner, copyright © 1976. Reprinted by permission of Little, Brown, an imprint of Hachette Book Group, Inc.

White, Christopher. Excerpts from "Prologue" from SKIPJACK by Christopher White. Copyright © 2009 by Christopher White. Reprinted by permission of St. Martin's Press. All Rights Reserved.

Wisner, Tom, and Mark Wisner. "Susquehanna Down." Printed with the permission of Mark Wisner.

SOURCES

"African Americans in the Chesapeake." Chesapeake Bay Program, www.chesapeakebay.net/discover/history/african-americans-in -the-chesapeake.

Bonner, Christopher. "Frederick Douglass's Radical Imagination." Black Perspectives, 26 November 2018, www.aaihs.org/frederick -douglasss-radical-imagination/.

Chen, Nancy, and Analisa Novak. "'Ghost Forests' Along US Coasts Are a Haunting Indicator of Climate Change." CBS News, 21 April 2023, www.cbsnews.com/news/ghost-forests-chesapeake -bay-us-coasts-climate-change/.

Davis, Joel. "Piscataway Indians Gather for First Time as 'Official' Tribe." *Washington Post*, 13 June 2012, www.washingtonpost.com /local/piscataway-indians-gather-for-first-time-as-official-tribe /2012/06/12/gJQAWpjoZV_story.html.

From Slavery to Freedom on the Patuxent. 2023. Calvert Marine Museum, Solomons, Maryland.

"The Ghost Forests of Blackwater National Wildlife Refuge." Alliance for the Chesapeake Bay, 28 October 2020, www.allianceforthebay .org/2020/10/the-ghost-forests-of-blackwater-national-wildlife -refuge/.

"Glossary of Blue Crab Biology." *Chesapeake Quarterly*, July 2012, www.chesapeakequarterly.net/V11N2/side4/index.html.

Harley, Mario. "Piscataway Exhibit." Historic London Town and Gardens, 5 December 2022, www.historiclondontown.org/post /piscataway-exhibit.

Havre de Grace's Role in the Underground Railroad. 2023. Havre de Grace Maritime Museum, Havre de Grace, Maryland.

Livie, Kate. "Cultivating Change." *Chesapeake Bay Magazine*, 4 November 2021.

Martin, Sandra Olivetti. "'Follow on the Water' Reviewed by Sandra Olivetti Martin." CHESTORY—The Center for the Chesapeake Story, chears.org/chestory/essays.htm.

"Maryland: Piscataway Park." National Park Service, www.nps.gov /articles/piscataway.htm.

Metcalf, A. J. "Partnership Adds 78 Oyster Reef Balls off Coast of Chesapeake Beach, Maryland." Chesapeake Bay Foundation, 29 July 2021, www.cbf.org/news-media/newsroom/2021/maryland /partnership-adds-78-oyster-reef-balls-off-coast-of-chesapeake -beach-maryland.html.

Minorities In Aquaculture, www.mianpo.org.

"Native Land." Native Land Digital, native-land.ca.

Oglesby, Cameron. "How Oysters Became a Source of Economic Freedom for Emancipated Black Folks." Earth in Color, 18 April

2022, earthincolor.co/earth-curiosity/how-oysters-became-a
-source-of-economic-freedom/.

"Oyster Restoration: Bringing Back an Icon to the Chesapeake Bay."
The Nature Conservancy, 10 April 2023, www.nature.org/en-us
/about-us/where-we-work/united-states/maryland-dc/stories
-in-maryland-dc/oyster-restoration-in-maryland/.

"Oysters." Chesapeake Bay Program, www.chesapeakebay.net/issues
/whats-at-risk/oysters.

Richardson, Chief Anne. "Life Along the Rappahannock: An Oral
History Program," 8 March 2018,https://www.youtube.com/watch?
v=UnfLuBg9bYs.

Savoy, Lauret. "Ancestral Structures on the Trailing Edge." *Emergence
Magazine,* 15 June 2023, https://emergencemagazine.org/essay
/ancestral-structures-on-the-trailing-edge/.

Shomette, Donald G. "The Ghost Fleet of Mallows Bay." Maryland
Department of Natural Resources, Winter 2001, dnr.maryland.gov
/ccs/Documents/GhostFleet-of-MallowsBay.pdf.

Tayac, Gabrielle. *Spirits in the River: A Report on the Piscataway People,*
for Smithsonian Institution, National Museum of the American
Indian, Washington DC, 1999.

Tayac, Gabrielle, and Edwin Schupman. *We Have A Story to Tell: The
Native Peoples of the Chesapeake Region*, Education Office of the
National Museum of the American Indian, Washington DC, 2006.

"What Is a Watershed?" The Chesapeake Bay Program,
www.chesapeakebay.net/discover/watershed.

"What Is an Estuary?" National Ocean Service, National Oceanic
and Atmospheric Administration, oceanservice.noaa.gov/facts
/estuary.html.

Wheeler, Timothy B. "Bernie Fowler, Tireless Maryland Advocate
for Clean Water, Dies." *Bay Journal,* 20 December 2021,
www.bayjournal.com/news/people/bernie-fowler-tireless
-maryland-advocate-for-clean-water-dies/article_2339a8b8-
5db5-11ec-a9db-ff97aa7dc242.html.

Directory

BAYWIDE

Captain John Smith Chesapeake National Historic Trail
nps.gov/cajo
Virginia, Maryland, Delaware, DC, Pennsylvania, New York

Chesapeake Bay Gateways and Water Trails Network
nps.gov/articles/chesapeake-gateways.htm

Cross Island Trail
traillink.com/trail/cross-island-trail
Maryland, from Long Point Park in Grasonville to Terrapin Nature Park in Stevensville

Harriet Tubman Underground Railroad Scenic Byway
harriettubmanbyway.org
Eastern Shore of Maryland to Delaware

Star-Spangled Banner National Historic Trail
nps.gov/stsp
Virginia, Maryland, DC

UPPER BAY

Conowingo Dam Visitor Center
visitmaryland.org/listing/visitor-centers/conowingo-visitor-center
4948 Conowingo Rd, Darlington, MD

Eastern Neck National Wildlife Refuge
fws.gov/refuge/eastern-neck
1730 Eastern Neck Rd, Rock Hall, MD

Elk Neck State Park
dnr.maryland.gov/publiclands/pages/central/elkneck.aspx
4395 Turkey Point Rd, North East, MD

Gunpowder Falls State Park, Hammerman Area
dnr.maryland.gov/publiclands/Pages/central/GunpowderFalls/Hammerman-Area.aspx
7200 Graces Quarters Rd, Middle River, MD

Marshy Point Nature Center
marshypoint.org
7130 Marshy Point Rd,
Middle River, MD

The Bookplate
thebookplate.net
112 S Cross St, Chestertown, MD

Tuckahoe State Park
dnr.maryland.gov/publiclands
/Pages/eastern/tuckahoe.aspx
13070 Crouse Mill Rd,
Queen Anne, MD

Turkey Point Lighthouse
dnr.maryland.gov/publiclands
/Pages/central/ElkNeck/Turkey
-Point-Lighthouse.aspx
Located in Elk Neck State Park

WESTERN SHORE

Annapolis, MD
visitannapolis.org
. . . .

Annapolis Maritime Museum and Park
amaritime.org
723 Second Street
(museum campus)
7300 Edgewood Rd
(park campus)

Boatyard Bar and Grill
boatyardbarandgrill.com
400 Fourth St

Blackwall Hitch
blackwallhitchannapolis.com
400 Sixth St

Cantler's Riverside Inn
cantlers.com
458 Forest Beach Rd

Old Fox Books and Coffeehouse
oldfoxbooks.com
35 Maryland Ave

Potomac River
. . . .

Mallows Bay-Potomac River National Marine Sanctuary
sanctuaries.noaa.gov/mallows
-potomac/visit/maps.html
Mallows Bay Park is the primary access point to the sanctuary and the Ghost Fleet.
1440 Wilson Landing Rd,
Nanjemoy, MD

Torpedo Factory Art Center
torpedofactory.org
105 N Union St,
Alexandria, VA

EASTERN SHORE

Chesapeake Bay Environmental Center
bayrestoration.org
600 Discovery Ln,
Grasonville, MD

Terrapin Nature Park
*qac.org/facilities/facility/details
/terrapinnaturepark-97*
191 Log Canoe Cir,
Stevensville, MD

Water's Edge Museum
watersedgemuseum.org
101 Mill St, Oxford, MD

Crisfield, MD
explorecrisfield.com
....

Crisfield City Dock
1200-1300 W Main St

Janes Island State Park
*dnr.maryland.gov/publiclands/
Pages/eastern/janesisland.aspx*
26280 Alfred J Lawson Dr

Smith Island Baking Company
smithislandcake.com
45 West Chesapeake Ave

Cape Charles, VA
capecharlesvirginiascape.com
....

**Cape Charles
Brewing Company**
capecharlesbrewing.com
2198 Stone Rd

Coastal Baking Co.
coastalbakingco.com
555 Mason Avenue

Kiptopeke State Park
*dcr.virginia.gov/state-parks
/kiptopeke*
3540 Kiptopeke Dr

Lemon Tree Gallery and Studio
lemontree.gallery
301 Mason Ave #3203

LOVEwork sculpture
*virginia.org/listing/lovework-in
-cape-charles/15178*
21 Bay Ave

Peach Street Books and Cafe
peachstreetbooks.com
401 Mason Ave

Chesapeake Bay Bridge-Tunnel
Scenic Overview
cbbt.com
Lankford Hwy (west side)

St. Michaels, MD
stmichaelsmd.com
....

Ava's Pizzeria and Wine Bar
avaspizzeria.com
409 S Talbot St

**Chesapeake Bay
Maritime Museum**
cbmm.org
213 North Talbot St

Eastern Shore Brewing
easternshorebrewing.com
605 South Talbot Street

Hooper Strait Lighthouse
*cbmm.org/hooper-strait
-lighthouse*
*Located at the Chesapeake Bay
Maritime Museum*

**Limoncello Italian Restaurant
and Wine Bar**
limoncellostmichaels.com
200 S Talbot St

Lyon Rum Distillery
lyonrum.com
103 East Marengo St

St. Michael's Winery
stmichaelswinery.com
609 South Talbot Street

The Crab Claw Restaurant
thecrabclaw.com
304 Burns St

Solomons, MD area

Calvert Cliffs State Park
*dnr.maryland.gov/publiclands
/Pages/southern/calvertcliffs.aspx*
10540 H. G. Trueman Rd,
Lusby, MD

Calvert Marine Museum
calvertmarinemuseum.com
14200 Solomons Island Rd

Flag Ponds Nature Park
*calvertcountymd.gov/1192/Flag
-Ponds-Nature-Park*
1525 Flag Ponds Parkway,
Lusby, MD

Point Lookout Lighthouse
*dnr.maryland.gov/publiclands
/Pages/southern/pointlookout.aspx*
10350 Point Lookout Rd,
Scotland, MD

**The Lighthouse
Restaurant and Dock Bar**
*lighthouserestaurantanddockbar
.com*
14636 Solomons Island Rd S

The Pier
thepiersolomons.com
14575 Solomons Island Rd

Easton, MD area
eastonmd.org

**Harriet Tubman
Underground Railroad
National Historical Park**
nps.gov/hatu
4068 Golden Hill Rd,
Church Creek, MD

**Blackwater National
Wildlife Refuge**
fws.gov/refuge/blackwater
2145 Key Wallace Drive,
Cambridge, MD

Flying Cloud Booksellers
flyingcloudbooks.com
26 West Dover St

Flying Cloud Fine Art Posters
24 West Dover St

Frederick Douglass Statue
Located outside the Talbot County Courthouse
11 N. Washington St

Pickering Creek Audubon Center
pickeringcreek.org
11450 Audubon Ln

Rise Up Coffee Roasters
riseupcoffee.com
618 Dover Rd

Havre de Grace, MD
explorehavredegrace.com

Concord Point Lighthouse
concordpointlighthouse.org
714 Concord St

Havre de Grace Decoy Museum
decoymuseum.com
215 Giles St

JoRetro Vintage Market
joretro.com
137 N Washington St

Seneca Cannery Antique Mall
facebook.com/p/Seneca-Cannery-Antiques-100063637240007
201 St John St

Susquehanna State Park
dnr.maryland.gov/publiclands/Pages/central/susquehanna.aspx
4118 Wilkinson Rd

BARRIER ISLANDS

Assateague Island National Seashore
nps.gov/asis/index.htm
7206 National Seashore Lane, Berlin, MD

Chincoteague National Wildlife Refuge
fws.gov/refuge/chincoteague
8231 Beach Rd, Chincoteague, VA

The Mermaid Museum
berlinmermaidmuseum.com
4 Jefferson St, Berlin, MD (Upstairs)

About the Contributors

Curtis J. Badger is a writer and photographer whose work focuses on the Eastern Shore of Virginia, his native coast. Books he has written include *Salt Tide: Cycles and Currents of Life Along the Coast* (1999), *A Naturalist's Guide to the Virginia Coast* (2004), *A Natural History of Quiet Waters: Swamps and Wetlands of the Mid-Atlantic Coast* (2007), and *Wilderness Regained: The Story of the Virginia Barrier Islands* (2nd edition, 2022).

Gilbert Byron (1903–1991) authored fourteen books and more than seventy short stories, poems, and articles detailing life on the Chesapeake Bay in the twentieth century, perhaps the largest collection of writings on the Chesapeake by one person. He was born in Chestertown, Maryland, a waterman's son, and lived on the Eastern Shore nearly all his life. The small cabin where he lived and wrote for decades is now part of Pickering Creek Audubon Center in Easton, Maryland.

Emily Decker is a Virginia native who was born on the Chesapeake, spent her childhood in Ghana, and lived during her growing-up years in Atlanta, Georgia. She holds a master's degree in education from Georgia State University, and her poetry has appeared in *Yellow Arrow Journal, Full Bleed,* and *Hole in the Head Review*. Emily currently resides in Baltimore, Maryland, where she loves to sail and explore the beauty and heritage of the Chesapeake Bay.

Christine Higgins is a McDowell Colony fellow and the recipient of Individual Artist Awards in Poetry and Non- Fiction from The Maryland State Arts Council. Her work has appeared in numerous print and online journals. Hello, Darling, won 2nd place in the Poetry Box chapbook competition in 2020. She is the author of Plum Point Folio, a collection of poems combined with her husband's wildlife photographs. Her full-length manuscript, I Iallow, was published in Spring 2020 by Cherry Grove Collections.

Annie Marhefka is a writer in Baltimore, Maryland whose recent publications have appeared in *Pithead Chapel, Reckon Review, Literary Mama, JMWW, Lunch Ticket,* and more. Her writing has been nominated for the Pushcart Prize and Best of the Net. Annie is the Executive Director at Yellow Arrow Publishing, a Baltimore-based nonprofit empowering women-identifying writers. She has a BA in creative writing from Washington College and an MBA. Annie's work has been supported by the Maryland State Arts Council and Gullklstan Center for the Arts.

James Michener (1907–1997) made a career of writing long fictional sagas spanning multiple generations, set in specific locations and incorporating rich historical detail. Many of his more than forty books were bestsellers, and all were based on meticulous research. His first book, *Tales of the South Pacific,* won the Pulitzer Prize for Fiction in 1948 and was adapted by Rodgers and Hammerstein as the Broadway musical *South Pacific*. Other notable works include *Hawaii* (1959) and *Centennial* (1974), set in the Rocky Mountains of Colorado.

Tiya Miles is Michael Garvey Professor of History at Harvard University and author of the 2024 book *Night Flyer: Harriet Tubman and the Faith Dreams of a Free People*, along with five prize-winning histories of American slavery. Miles's other recent works include the 2021 National Book Award winner *All That She Carried: The Journey of Ashley's Sack, a Black Family Keepsake*, and her 2023 book *Wild Girls: How the Outdoors Shaped the Women Who Challenged a Nation*. Miles was awarded a MacArthur Fellowship in 2011.

Lara Payne teaches writing and is a student of anthropology, archeology, and poetry who is interested in how humans interact with the Chesapeake, how it affects us, and how we affect it. Payne's understanding of the Chesapeake is informed by her time traveling and camping around the Bay growing up, paddling canoes and kayaks on its many tributaries, interviewing oystermen in St. Mary's County, and sailing on a reconstructed seventeenth-century trading ship called the *Maryland Dove*.

RagghiRain is a well-known Native American storyteller and the resident storyteller at the Nanticoke Indian Museum in Millsboro, Delaware. Of Eastern Cherokee descent, Rain serves on the executive committee of the Native American International Caucus of the United Methodist Church.

Audrey Y. Scharmen (1927–2017) had lived in arid places. Her childhood home was Dustbowl Kansas during the Great Depression and her marriage to military pilot Merrill left her, often alone with her growing family, in deserts. As Merrill aged out of flying and moved up the hierarchy, Audrey played a more public role of military wife, and they later retired to Chesapeake Country, where she found her muse. Here, she wrote, "she reaffirmed her earliest vows in odes to the gentle side of nature. She saw, she listened, and she has never ceased."

Donald G. Shomette is an internationally recognized expert in maritime history and underwater archaeology who has specialized in the history of the Chesapeake Bay. Author of more than twenty books, he has worked extensively with the Library of Congress, the National Geographic Society, and the National Park Service. Shomette is an amateur diver and has a particular fascination with pirates and shipwrecks.

MaKshya Tolbert is a writer and poet whose work has appeared in *Narrative* magazine, *Emergence Magazine, Tupelo Quarterly, RHINO, Art Papers*, and *Odd Apples*. Tolbert received their MFA in poetry from the University of Virginia and serves on the Charlottesville Tree Commission.

William Warner (1920–2008) was an author who spent most of his life living and working in the Chesapeake Bay area. After serving in the Naval Reserve in World War II, he went on to work for the United States Information Agency and the Smithsonian Institution. An avid sailor and nature enthusiast, he won a Pulitzer Prize for Nonfiction in 1977 for *Beautiful Swimmers*, blending history, ecology, and anthropology through poetic prose to tell the story of the underwater lives of blue crabs and the profession of those who catch them.

Christopher White is a science writer and naturalist who grew up on the shores of the Chesapeake Bay. He is the author of several books in addition to *Skipjack*—including *The Melting World: A Journey Across America's Vanishing Glaciers* and *The Last Lobster: Boom or Bust for Maine's Greatest Fishery?*—and has written articles for publications like *Audubon,* the *Baltimore Sun,* and *National Geographic.* White is also a filmmaker and producer of *The Blue Revolution*, an eight-part television documentary on humans' relationship with the sea that was broadcast on the Discovery Channel.

Mark Wisner, son of Tom Wisner, spent his childhood playing by the water, chasing the crabs, fish, and other critters found in the Chesapeake Bay. Due in large part to his father's stories of the watermen, he spent two winters dredging oysters on Maryland's sailing skipjacks. Today, Mark has continued that legacy on the water to commercial fishing in Alaska. His five children have all worked as fishermen, and the stories and the beauty of the Bay have carried on into their eyes.

Tom Wisner (1930–2010) was born in Washington DC and spent time with his family along the James River in the Chesapeake Bay watershed as a child. With a degree in biology and graduate work in ecology, he served for decades as an educator with the University of Maryland's Chesapeake Biological Laboratory. At the same time, he established himself as a writer and singer of songs about the plant and animal life of the Chesapeake Bay, hoping to help people develop a new relationship with the Bay.

About the Editors

Ilyssa Kyu is the founder of Amble, a sabbatical program for creative professionals to take time away with purpose in support of nature conservancies. She is a design researcher and strategist with a degree in industrial design and previously worked at boutique and global design studios. She is currently using her design consulting experience to support nature nonprofits through All Hands, a creative collective, as well as continually dreaming up ways to integrate her love for storytelling and the outdoors.

Dave Kyu is a socially engaged artist and writer. Born in Seoul, South Korea, and raised in the United States, he explores the creative tensions of identity, community, and public space in his work. He has managed public arts projects for the Asian Arts Initiative, Mural Arts, and the City of Philadelphia. His own creative projects have found him commissioning skywriting planes to write messages 10,000 feet above Philadelphia and doing everything Facebook told him to do for a month.

Together, they've created the *Campfire Stories* book and card deck series.They were artists-in-residence at Independence National Historical Park in Philadelphia, PA—a collaboration between the NEA, the National Park Service, and the Mural Arts Program—which resulted in an event, "I Will Hold You in the Light," which brought together six diverse performers responding to the theme of "The Pursuit of Happiness."